Guitar
Advanced
Chords

Easy-to-Use, Easy-to-Carry
One Chord on EVERY Page

Jake Jackson

FLAME TREE
PUBLISHING

Produced and created by
FLAME TREE PUBLISHING
6 Melbray Mews, Fulham,
London, SW6 3NS
United Kingdom
www.flametreepublishing.com

See our music information site:
www.FlameTreeMusic.com

First Published in 2010

Publisher & Creative Director: Nick Wells
Editors: Polly Prior and Sara Robson
Designer: Jake

21 23 25 24 22

7 9 10 8

ISBN: 978-1-84786-949-4

Printed in China

Introduction

The identification, understanding and use of new chords is an essential part of every guitarist's toolkit. Each chord can be expressed in a number of different ways but we have chosen a simple range of hand positions that will quickly enable you to capture the flavour of the music. The book offers one chord per page with a variety of hand positions and fingerings for hundreds of chords.

Tabs on the side of each page help you explore each key

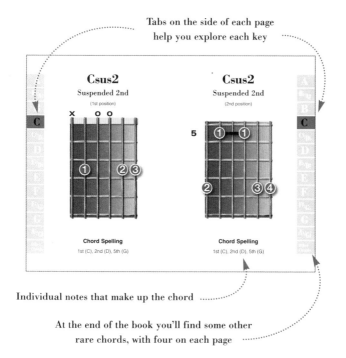

Individual notes that make up the chord

At the end of the book you'll find some other rare chords, with four on each page

Simple Guide to the Chord Boxes

The chord fretboxes in this book provide a useful companion to more introductory chord resources, including our own, best-selling *Guitar Chords* book.

Many of the advanced chord resources available take little account of the actual fingering necessary so we have worked hard to provide two hand positions for a selection of advanced voicings that can be used alongside more simple chords, allowing you to create the building blocks for interesting new sounds, songs and instrumentals. We have used a number of different hand positions but they can, of course, be adapted to a different key by moving up and down the neck.

- The chords are divided by key, from A to G♯, with the chord's notes (spelling) shown at the bottom of the page. The left-hand pages outline the main chords you will need to learn, shown in the first position.

- The right-hand pages give a second position of each chord. This can be handy when playing progressions, for linking chords or for use in improvisations. For the majority of the book we've only provided two positions in order to include a greater variety of chords.

- The diagrams show the guitar fretboard in an upright position, with high E on the right. The nut appears at the top if the chord is played on the lower frets. If the chord is in a higher position, the fret number on which it begins is given to the left of the diagram.

- At the end of the book we have provided four extra chords for each key, shown in the first position. Also, as a useful additional resource, the last few pages show the major scale spelling for each key.

- The notes to be played are shown as circles, with the finger number that should be used for each note (❶ = index finger; ❷ = middle finger; ❸ = ring finger; ❹ = little finger). An **X** above the string indicates that the string should not be played in the chord and should be muted, to prevent it sounding accidentally. An **O** above the string shows that it should be played as an open string.

- We have tried to make this chord section as easy to use as possible, so where there is a choice of note name (e.g. F♯ or G♭) we have selected the one that you are most likely to come across in your playing.

- Where a chord contains a flattened (♭) or sharpened (♯) interval (e.g. ♯5th), you can find the notes by playing a fret lower (for a flat) or a fret higher (for a sharp) than the interval note indicated at the top of the page. In the keys that contain a large number of sharps or flats, double flats (♭♭) and double sharps (x) sometimes occur in the augmented and diminished chords. A double flat is the notes two frets below the named note, while a double sharp is two frets up.

An X at the top of a string indicates that this string should not be played

An O at the top of the string means that this should be played as an open string

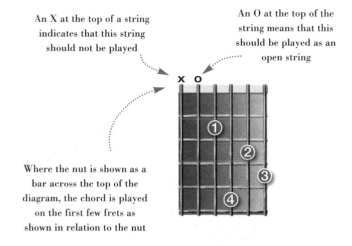

Where the nut is shown as a bar across the top of the diagram, the chord is played on the first few frets as shown in relation to the nut

Where a bar appears between notes, the specified finger should hold down the notes across the strings shown

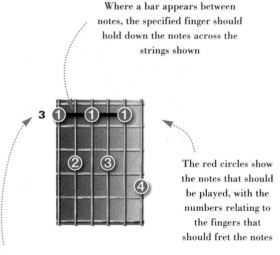

The red circles show the notes that should be played, with the numbers relating to the fingers that should fret the notes

Where the chord is to be played in a different position, the fret number is shown to the left of the diagram

A

Asus2
Suspended 2nd
(1st position)

Chord Spelling

1st (A), 2nd (B), 5th (E)

Asus2

Suspended 2nd

(2nd position)

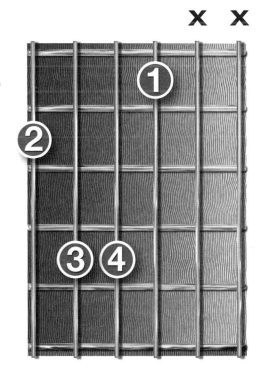

4

x x

Chord Spelling

1st (A), 2nd (B), 5th (E)

A

B♭/A♯

B

C

C♯/D♭

D

E♭/D♯

E

F

F♯/G♭

G

A♭/G♯

Other Chords

Amaj11

Major 11th

(1st position)

Chord Spelling

1st (A), 3rd (C♯), 5th (E), 7th (G♯), 9th (B), 11th (D)

Amaj11
Major 11th
(2nd position)

A
B♭/A♯
B
C
C♯/D♭
D
E♭/D♯
E
F
F♯/G♭
G
A♭/G♯
Other Chords

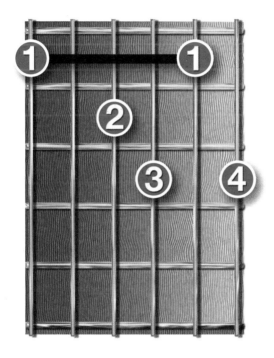

5

Chord Spelling

1st (A), 3rd (C♯), 5th (E), 7th (G♯),
9th (B), 11th (D)

Am11

Minor 11th

(1st position)

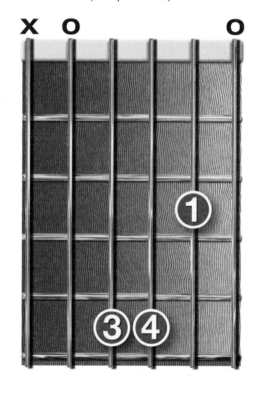

Chord Spelling

1st (A), ♭3rd (C), 5th (E), ♭7th (G),
9th (B), 11th (D)

Am11

Minor 11th

(2nd position)

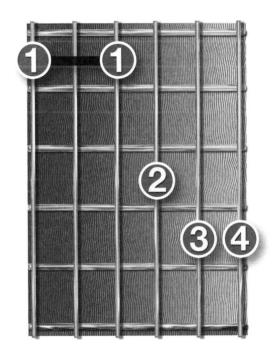

5

A

B♭/A♯

B

C

C♯/D♭

D

E♭/D♯

E

F

F♯/G♭

G

A♭/G♯

Other Chords

Chord Spelling

1st (A), ♭3rd (C), 5th (E), ♭7th (G),
9th (B), 11th (D)

A

B♭/A♯

B

C

C♯/D♭

D

E♭/D♯

E

F

F♯/G♭

G

A♭/G♯

Other Chords

Am maj11
Minor Major 11th

(1st position)

Chord Spelling

1st (A), ♭3rd (C), 5th (E), 7th (G♯)
9th (B), 11th (D)

Am maj11
Minor Major 11th
(2nd position)

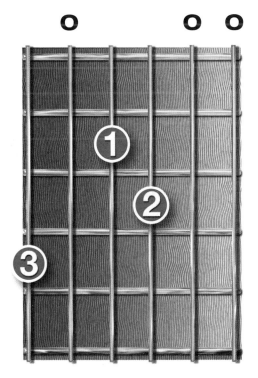

5

A
B♭/A♯
B
C
C♯/D♭
D
E♭/D♯
E
F
F♯/G♭
G
A♭/G♯
Other Chords

Chord Spelling

1st (A), ♭3rd (C), 5th (E), 7th (G♯)
9th (B), 11th (D)

Amaj13

Major 13th

(1st position)

Chord Spelling

1st (A), 3rd (C♯), 5th (E), 7th (G♯)
9th (B), 11th (D), 13th (F♯)

Amaj13
Major 13th
(2nd position)

4

Chord Spelling

1st (A), 3rd (C♯), 5th (E), 7th (G♯)
9th (B), 11th (D), 13th (F♯)

Am13

Minor 13th

(1st position)

Chord Spelling

1st (A), ♭3rd (C), 5th (E), ♭7th (G)
9th (B), 11th (D), 13th (F♯)

A

B♭/A♯

B

C

C♯/D♭

D

E♭/D♯

E

F

F♯/G♭

G

A♭/G♯

Other Chords

Am13

Minor 13th

(2nd position)

A

B♭/A♯

B

C

C♯/D♭

D

E♭/D♯

E

F

F♯/G♭

G

A♭/G♯

Other
Chords

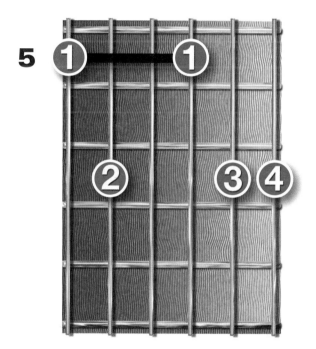

5

Chord Spelling

1st (A), ♭3rd (C), 5th (E), ♭7th (G)
9th (B), 11th (D), 13th (F♯)

Am maj13
Minor Major 13th

(1st position)

A

B♭/A♯

B

C

C♯/D♭

D

E♭/D♯

E

F

F♯/G♭

G

A♭/G♯

Other Chords

Chord Spelling

1st (A), ♭3rd (C), 5th (E), 7th (G♯)
9th (B), 11th (D), 13th (F♯)

Am maj13

Minor Major 13th

(2nd position)

A
Bb/A#
B
C
C#/Db
D
Eb/D#
E
F
F#/Gb
G
Ab/G#
Other Chords

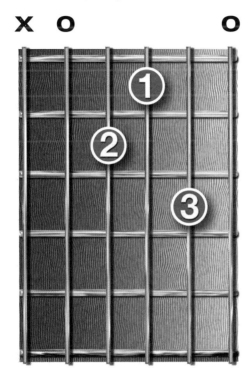

Chord Spelling

1st (A), b3rd (C), 5th (E), 7th (G#)
9th (B), 11th (D), 13th (F#)

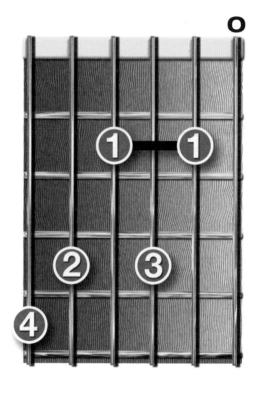

A+9

Major Add 9th

(1st position)

Chord Spelling

1st (A), 3rd (C♯), 5th (E), 9th (B)

A
B♭/A♯
B
C
C♯/D♭
D
E♭/D♯
E
F
F♯/G♭
G
A♭/G♯
Other Chords

A+9

Major Add 9th

(2nd position)

X

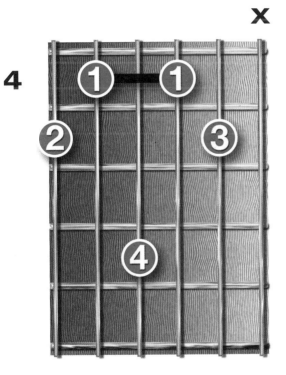

4

A

B♭/A♯

B

C

C♯/D♭

D

E♭/D♯

E

F

F♯/G♭

G

A♭/G♯

Other Chords

Chord Spelling

1st (A), 3rd (C♯), 5th (E), 9th (B)

A

B♭/A♯

B

C

C♯/D♭

D

E♭/D♯

E

F

F♯/G♭

G

A♭/G♯

Other Chords

Am+9

Minor Add 9th

(1st position)

Chord Spelling

1st (A), ♭3rd (C), 5th (E), 9th (B)

Am+9

Minor Add 9th

(2nd position)

A

Bb/A#

B

C

C#/Db

D

Eb/D#

E

F

F#/Gb

G

Ab/G#

Other Chords

5

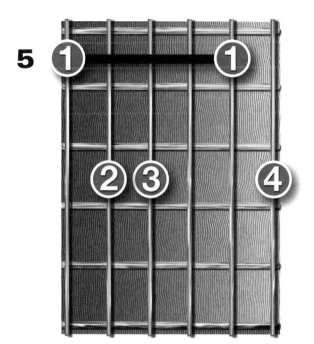

Chord Spelling

1st (A), ♭3rd (C), 5th (E), 9th (B)

Am6+9

Minor 6th Add 9th

(1st position)

Chord Spelling

1st (A), ♭3rd (C), 5th (E), 6th (F♯)
9th (B)

Am6+9

Minor 6th Add 9th

(2nd position)

X X

5

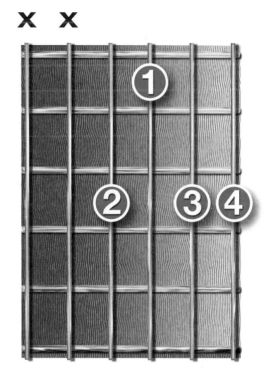

Chord Spelling

1st (A), ♭3rd (C), 5th (E), 6th (F♯)
9th (B)

A

B♭/A♯

B

C

C♯/D♭

D

E♭/D♯

E

F

F♯/G♭

G

A♭/G♯

Other Chords

A7+9

7th Add 9th

(1st position)

Chord Spelling

1st (A), 3rd (C♯), 5th (E), 7th (G♯)
9th (B)

A7+9

7th Add 9th

(2nd position)

5

A

B♭/A♯

B

C

C♯/D♭

D

E♭/D♯

E

F

F♯/G♭

G

A♭/G♯

Other Chords

Chord Spelling

1st (A), 3rd (C♯), 5th (E), 7th (G♯)
9th (B)

B♭/A♯
B
C
C♯/D♭
D
E♭/D♯
E
F
F♯/G♭
G
A♭/G♯
Other Chords

A6sus4

6th Suspended 4th

(1st position)

Chord Spelling

1st (A), 4th (D), 5th (E), 6th (F♯)

A6sus4

6th Suspended 4th

(2nd position)

Chord Spelling

1st (A), 4th (D), 5th (E), 6th (F♯)

Amaj7sus4

Major 7th Suspended 4th

(1st position)

Chord Spelling

1st (A), 4th (D), 5th (E), 7th (G♯)

Amaj7sus4

Major 7th Suspended 4th

(2nd position)

A

Bb/A#

B

C

C#/Db

D

Eb/D#

E

F

F#/Gb

G

Ab/G#

Other Chords

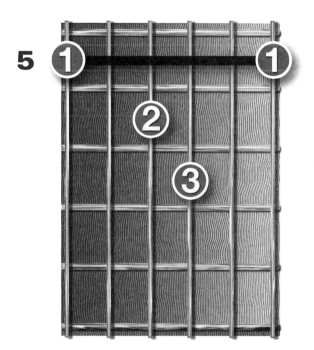

5

Chord Spelling

1st (A), 4th (D), 5th (E), 7th (G#)

Amaj9sus4

Major 9th Suspended 4th

(1st position)

B♭/A♯
B
C
C♯/D♭
D
E♭/D♯
E
F
F♯/G♭
G
A♭/G♯
Other
Chords

Chord Spelling

1st (A), 4th (D), 5th (E), 7th (G♯)
9th (B)

Amaj9sus4
Major 9th Suspended 4th
(2nd position)

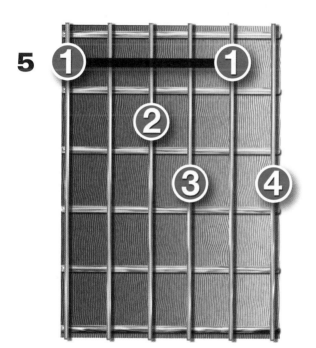

5

Chord Spelling

1st (A), 4th (D), 5th (E), 7th (G♯)
9th (B)

A9sus4

9th Suspended 4th

(1st position)

Chord Spelling

1st (A), 4th (D), 5th (E), ♭7th (G)
9th (B)

A9sus4

9th Suspended 4th

(2nd position)

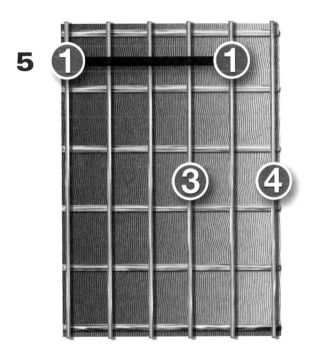

5

A

B♭/A♯

B

C

C♯/D♭

D

E♭/D♯

E

F

F♯/G♭

G

A♭/G♯

Other Chords

Chord Spelling

1st (A), 4th (D), 5th (E), ♭7th (G)
9th (B)

A

B♭/A♯

B

C

C♯/D♭

D

E♭/D♯

E

F

F♯/G♭

G

A♭/G♯

Other
Chords

B♭sus2

Suspended 2nd

(1st position)

Chord Spelling

1st (B♭), 2nd (C), 5th (F)

B♭sus2

Suspended 2nd

(2nd position)

X   X

5

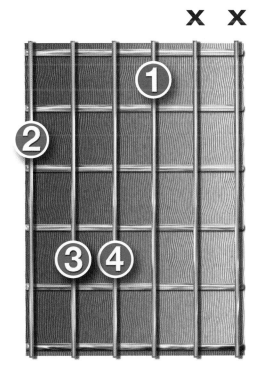

A

B♭/A♯

B

C

C♯/D♭

D

E♭/D♯

E

F

F♯/G♭

G

A♭/G♯

Other Chords

Chord Spelling

1st (B♭), 2nd (C), 5th (F)

A

B♭/A#

B

C

C#/D♭

D

E♭/D#

E

F

F#/G♭

G

A♭/G#

Other
Chords

B♭maj11

Major 11th

(1st position)

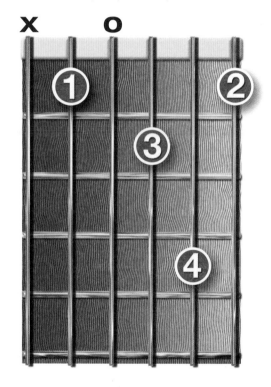

Chord Spelling

1st (B♭), 3rd (D), 5th (F), 7th (A),
9th (C), 11th (E♭)

B♭maj11
Major 11th
(2nd position)

X X

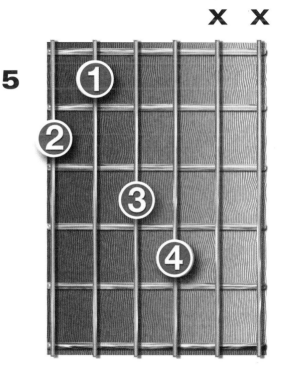

5

A
B♭/A♯
B
C
C♯/D♭
D
E♭/D♯
E
F
F♯/G♭
G
A♭/G♯
Other Chords

Chord Spelling

1st (B♭), 3rd (D), 5th (F), 7th (A),
9th (C), 11th (E♭)

B♭m11

Minor 11th

(1st position)

A

B♭/A♯

B

C

C♯/D♭

D

E♭/D♯

E

F

F♯/G♭

G

A♭/G♯

Other Chords

4

Chord Spelling

1st (B♭), ♭3rd (D♭), 5th (F), ♭7th (A♭),
9th (C), 11th (E♭)

B♭m11

Minor 11th

(2nd position)

A

B♭/A♯

B

C

C♯/D♭

D

E♭/D♯

E

F

F♯/G♭

G

A♭/G♯

Other
Chords

6

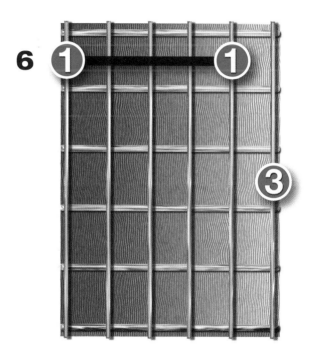

Chord Spelling

1st (B♭), ♭3rd (D♭), 5th (F), ♭7th (A♭),
9th (C), 11th (E♭)

B♭m maj11
Minor Major 11th
(1st position)

X

4

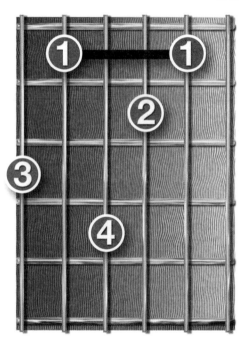

Chord Spelling

1st (B♭), ♭3rd (D♭), 5th (F), 7th (A)
9th (C), 11th (E♭)

B♭m maj11

Minor Major 11th

(2nd position)

A

B♭/A♯

B

C

C♯/D♭

D

E♭/D♯

E

F

F♯/G♭

G

A♭/G♯

Other Chords

X

11

Chord Spelling

1st (B♭), ♭3rd (D♭), 5th (F), 7th (A)
9th (C), 11th (E♭)

B♭maj13

Major 13th

(1st position)

Chord Spelling

1st (B♭), 3rd (D), 5th (F), 7th (A)
9th (C), 11th (E♭), 13th (G)

B♭maj13

Major 13th

(2nd position)

A

B♭/A#

B

C

C#/D♭

D

E♭/D#

E

F

F#/G♭

G

A♭/G#

Other
Chords

5

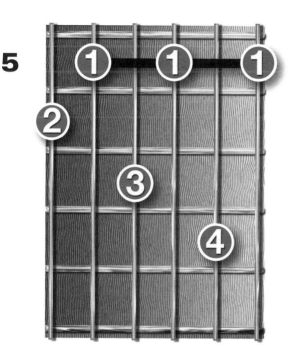

Chord Spelling

1st (B♭), 3rd (D), 5th (F), 7th (A)
9th (C), 11th (E♭), 13th (G)

B♭m13

Minor 13th

(1st position)

A

B♭/A#

B

C

C#/D♭

D

E♭/D#

E

F

F#/G♭

G

A♭/G#

Other Chords

Chord Spelling

1st (B♭), ♭3rd (D♭), 5th (F), ♭7th (A♭)
9th (C), 11th (E♭), 13th (G)

B♭m13

Minor 13th

(2nd position)

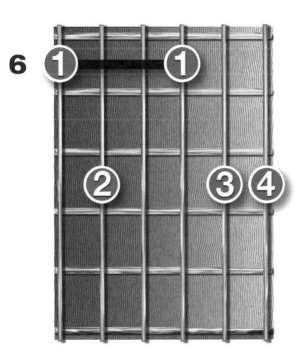

6

Chord Spelling

1st (B♭), ♭3rd (D♭), 5th (F), ♭7th (A♭)
9th (C), 11th (E♭), 13th (G)

B♭m maj13

Minor Major 13th

(1st position)

Chord Spelling

1st (B♭), ♭3rd (D♭), 5th (F), 7th (A)
9th (C), 11th (E♭), 13th (G)

B♭m maj13

Minor Major 13th

(2nd position)

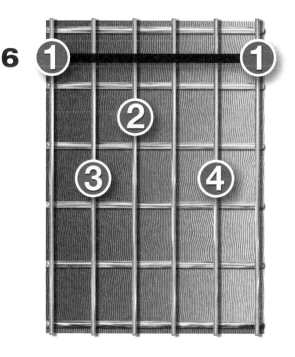

6

Chord Spelling

1st (B♭), ♭3rd (D♭), 5th (F), 7th (A)
9th (C), 11th (E♭), 13th (G)

B♭+9

Major Add 9th

(1st position)

Chord Spelling

1st (B♭), 3rd (D), 5th (F), 9th (C)

B♭+9

Major Add 9th

(2nd position)

A

B♭/A♯

B

C

C♯/D♭

D

E♭/D♯

E

F

F♯/G♭

G

A♭/G♯

Other Chords

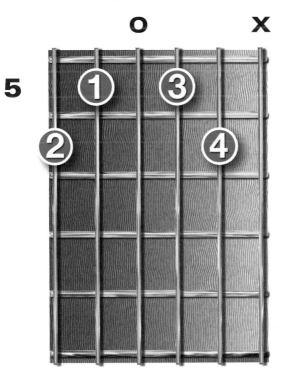

O   X

5

Chord Spelling

1st (B♭), 3rd (D), 5th (F), 9th (C)

B♭m+9

Minor Add 9th

(1st position)

X   **O**

Chord Spelling

1st (B♭), ♭3rd (D♭), 5th (F), 9th (C)

B♭m+9

Minor Add 9th

(2nd position)

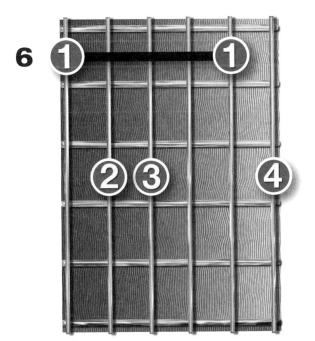

6

A

B♭/A#

B

C

C#/D♭

D

E♭/D#

E

F

F#/G♭

G

A♭/G#

Other Chords

Chord Spelling

1st (B♭), ♭3rd (D♭), 5th (F), 9th (C)

A

B♭/A♯

B

C

C♯/D♭

D

E♭/D♯

E

F

F♯/G♭

G

A♭/G♯

Other
Chords

B♭m6+9

Minor 6th Add 9th

(1st position)

X

4

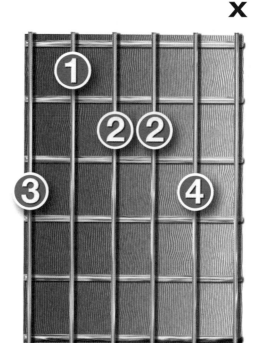

Chord Spelling

1st (B♭), ♭3rd (D♭), 5th (F), 6th (G)
9th (C)

B♭m6+9

Minor 6th Add 9th

(2nd position)

Chord Spelling

1st (B♭), ♭3rd (D♭), 5th (F), 6th (G)
9th (C)

A

B♭/A♯

B

C

C♯/D♭

D

E♭/D♯

E

F

F♯/G♭

G

A♭/G♯

Other
Chords

B♭7+9

7th Add 9th

(1st position)

Chord Spelling

1st (B♭), 3rd (D), 5th (F), 7th (A)
9th (C)

B♭7+9

7th Add 9th

(2nd position)

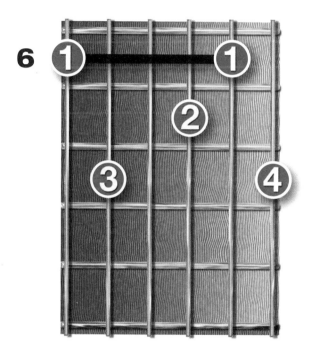

6

Chord Spelling

1st (B♭), 3rd (D), 5th (F), 7th (A)
9th (C)

A

B♭/A♯

B

C

C♯/D♭

D

E♭/D♯

E

F

F♯/G♭

G

A♭/G♯

Other Chords

B♭6sus4

6th Suspended 4th

(1st position)

X

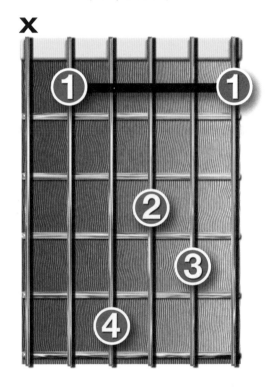

Chord Spelling

1st (B♭), 4th (E♭), 5th (F), 6th (G)

B♭6sus4

6th Suspended 4th

(2nd position)

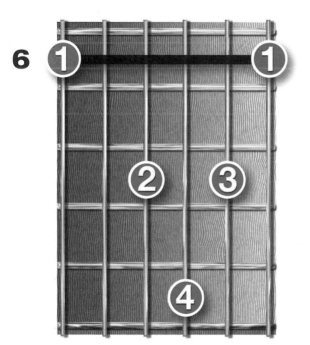

A
B♭/A♯
B
C
C♯/D♭
D
E♭/D♯
E
F
F♯/G♭
G
A♭/G♯
Other Chords

Chord Spelling

1st (B♭), 4th (E♭), 5th (F), 6th (G)

B♭maj7sus4

Major 7th Suspended 4th

(1st position)

Chord Spelling

1st (B♭), 4th (E♭), 5th (F), 7th (A)

B♭maj7sus4
Major 7th Suspended 4th
(2nd position)

A

B♭/A#

B

C

C#/D♭

D

E♭/D#

E

F

F#/G♭

G

A♭/G#

Other Chords

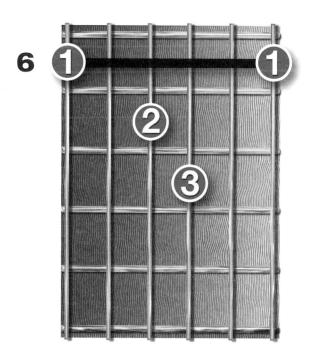

6

Chord Spelling
1st (B♭), 4th (E♭), 5th (F), 7th (A)

B♭maj9sus4

Major 9th Suspended 4th

(1st position)

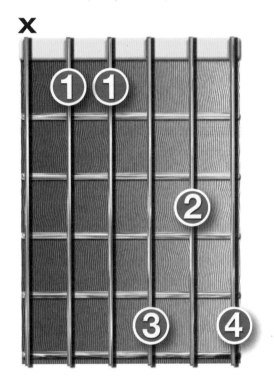

Chord Spelling

1st (B♭), 4th (E♭), 5th (F), 7th (A)
9th (C)

B♭maj9sus4
Major 9th Suspended 4th
(2nd position)

A

B♭/A#

B

C

C#/D♭

D

E♭/D#

E

F

F#/G♭

G

A♭/G#

Other Chords

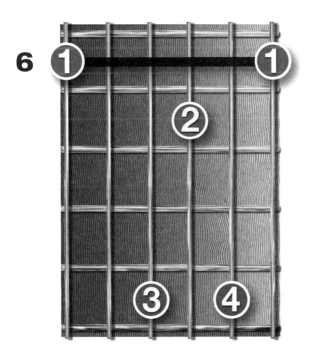

6

Chord Spelling
1st (B♭), 4th (E♭), 5th (F), 7th (A)
9th (C)

B♭9sus4

9th Suspended 4th

(1st position)

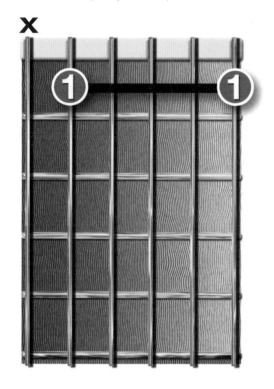

Chord Spelling

1st (B♭), 4th (E♭), 5th (F), ♭7th (A♭)
9th (C)

B♭9sus4

9th Suspended 4th

(2nd position)

A

B♭/A#

B

C

C#/D♭

D

E♭/D#

E

F

F#/G♭

G

A♭/G#

Other Chords

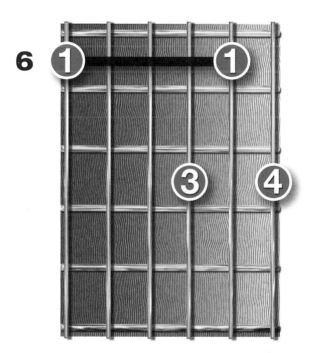

6

Chord Spelling

1st (B♭), 4th (E♭), 5th (F), ♭7th (A♭)
9th (C)

Bsus2

Suspended 2nd

(1st position)

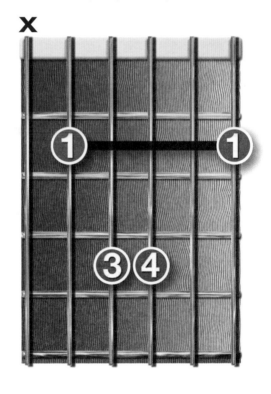

Chord Spelling

1st (B), 2nd (C#), 5th (F#)

Bsus2

Suspended 2nd

(2nd position)

X   X

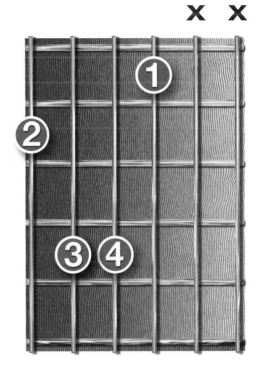

6

A

B♭/A♯

B

C

C♯/D♭

D

E♭/D♯

E

F

F♯/G♭

G

A♭/G♯

Other Chords

Chord Spelling

1st (B), 2nd (C♯), 5th (F♯)

Bmaj11
Major 11th
(1st position)

Chord Spelling

1st (B), 3rd (D#), 5th (F#), 7th (A#),
9th (C#), 11th (E)

Bmaj11
Major 11th
(2nd position)

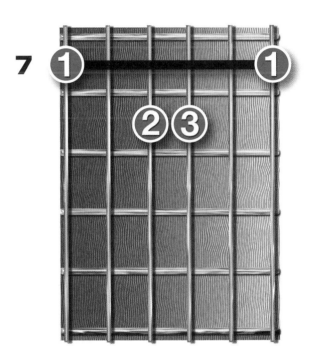

A
Bb/A#
B
C
C#/Db
D
Eb/D#
E
F
F#/Gb
G
Ab/G#
Other Chords

7

Chord Spelling

1st (B), 3rd (D♯), 5th (F♯), 7th (A♯),
9th (C♯), 11th (E)

Bm11

Minor 11th

(1st position)

X · O · O

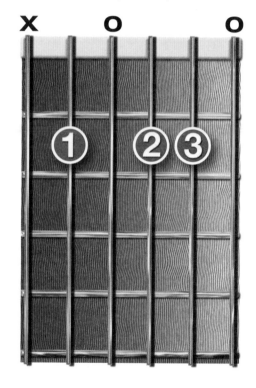

Chord Spelling

1st (B), ♭3rd (D), 5th (F♯), ♭7th (A),
9th (C♯), 11th (E)

A

B♭/A♯

B

C

C♯/D♭

D

E♭/D♯

E

F

F♯/G♭

G

A♭/G♯

Other
Chords

Bm11

Minor 11th

(2nd position)

A

B♭/A♯

B

C

C♯/D♭

D

E♭/D♯

E

F

F♯/G♭

G

A♭/G♯

Other
Chords

5

Chord Spelling

1st (B), ♭3rd (D), 5th (F♯), ♭7th (A),
9th (C♯), 11th (E)

Bm maj11
Minor Major 11th

(1st position)

Chord Spelling

1st (B), ♭3rd (D), 5th (F♯), 7th (A♯)
9th (C♯), 11th (E)

Bm maj11
Minor Major 11th
(2nd position)

A

B♭/A♯

B

C

C♯/D♭

D

E♭/D♯

E

F

F♯/G♭

G

A♭/G♯

Other Chords

X

5

Chord Spelling

1st (B), ♭3rd (D), 5th (F♯), 7th (A♯)
9th (C♯), 11th (E)

Bmaj13

Major 13th

(1st position)

Chord Spelling

1st (B), 3rd (D#), 5th (F#), 7th (A#)
9th (C#), 11th (E), 13th (G#)

Bmaj13
Major 13th
(2nd position)

A

B♭/A♯

B

C

C♯/D♭

D

E♭/D♯

E

F

F♯/G♭

G

A♭/G♯

Other Chords

6

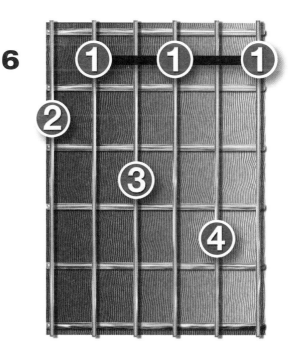

Chord Spelling

1st (B), 3rd (D♯), 5th (F♯), 7th (A♯)
9th (C♯), 11th (E), 13th (G♯)

Bm13

Minor 13th

(1st position)

Chord Spelling

1st (B), ♭3rd (D), 5th (F♯), ♭7th (A)
9th (C♯), 11th (E), 13th (G♯)

Bm13

Minor 13th

(2nd position)

A

B♭/A♯

B

C

C♯/D♭

D

E♭/D♯

E

F

F♯/G♭

G

A♭/G♯

Other Chords

7

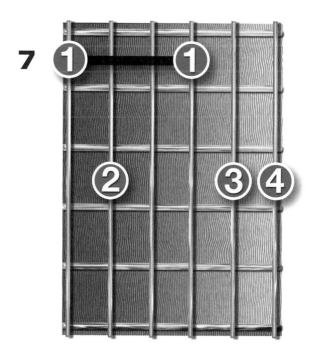

Chord Spelling

1st (B), ♭3rd (D), 5th (F♯), ♭7th (A)
9th (C♯), 11th (E), 13th (G♯)

Bm maj13
Minor Major 13th

(1st position)

Chord Spelling

1st (B), ♭3rd (D), 5th (F♯), 7th (A♯)
9th (C♯), 11th (E), 13th (G♯)

Bm maj13
Minor Major 13th
(2nd position)

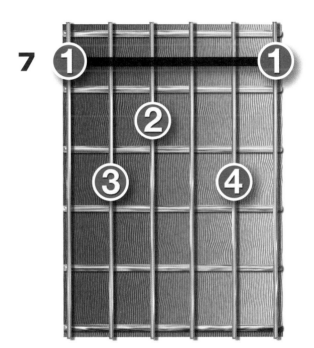

7

A

B♭/A♯

B

C

C♯/D♭

D

E♭/D♯

E

F

F♯/G♭

G

A♭/G♯

Other Chords

Chord Spelling

1st (B), ♭3rd (D), 5th (F♯), 7th (A♯)
9th (C♯), 11th (E), 13th (G♯)

B+9

Major Add 9th

(1st position)

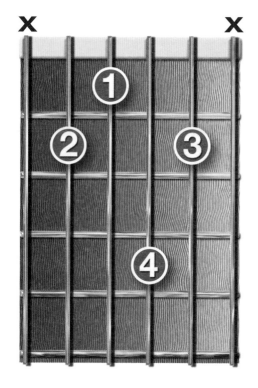

Chord Spelling

1st (B), 3rd (D♯), 5th (F♯), 9th (C♯)

A

B♭/A♯

B

C

C♯/D♭

D

E♭/D♯

E

F

F♯/G♭

G

A♭/G♯

Other Chords

B+9

Major Add 9th

(2nd position)

X

4

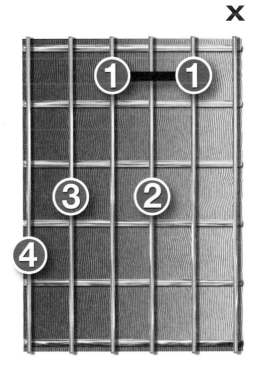

Chord Spelling

1st (B), 3rd (D♯), 5th (F♯), 9th (C♯)

A♭
B♭/A♯
B
C
C♯/D♭
D
E♭/D♯
E
F
F♯/G♭
G
A♭/G♯
Other Chords

Bm+9

Minor Add 9th

(1st position)

A

B♭/A♯

B

C

C♯/D♭

D

E♭/D♯

E

F

F♯/G♭

G

A♭/G♯

Other
Chords

X   O

Chord Spelling

1st (B), ♭3rd (D), 5th (F♯), 9th (C♯)

Bm+9

Minor Add 9th

(2nd position)

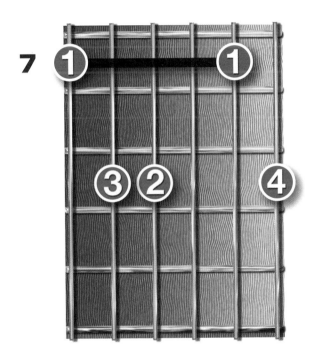

7

A

B♭/A♯

B

C

C♯/D♭

D

E♭/D♯

E

F

F♯/G♭

G

A♭/G♯

Other Chords

Chord Spelling

1st (B), ♭3rd (D), 5th (F♯), 9th (C♯)

Bm6+9

Minor 6th Add 9th

(1st position)

x   o

Chord Spelling

1st (B), ♭3rd (D), 5th (F♯), 6th (G♯)
9th (C♯)

Bm6+9

Minor 6th Add 9th

(2nd position)

X

5

A
B♭/A♯
B
C
C♯/D♭
D
E♭/D♯
E
F
F♯/G♭
G
A♭/G♯
Other Chords

Chord Spelling

1st (B), ♭3rd (D), 5th (F♯), 6th (G♯)
9th (C♯)

B7+9

7th Add 9th

(1st position)

X

Chord Spelling

1st (B), 3rd (D♯), 5th (F♯), 7th (A♯)
9th (C♯)

B7+9

7th Add 9th

(2nd position)

A

B♭/A♯

B

C

C♯/D♭

D

E♭/D♯

E

F

F♯/G♭

G

A♭/G♯

Other Chords

7

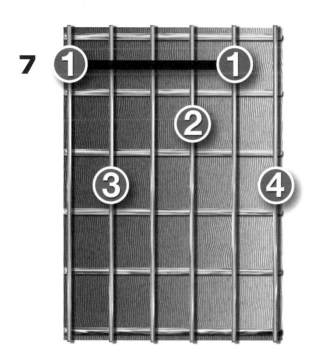

Chord Spelling

1st (B), 3rd (D♯), 5th (F♯), 7th (A♯)
9th (C♯)

B6sus4

6th Suspended 4th

(1st position)

X   O

① ② ③ ④

Chord Spelling

1st (B), 4th (E), 5th (F♯), 6th (G♯)

B6sus4

6th Suspended 4th

(2nd position)

X X

6

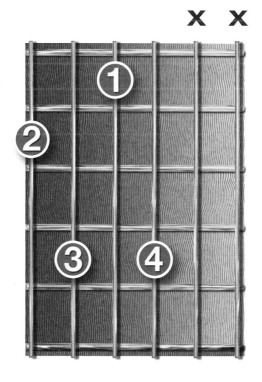

A
B♭/A♯
B
C♯/D♭
D
E♭/D♯
E
F
F♯/G♭
G
A♭/G♯
Other Chords

Chord Spelling

1st (B), 4th (E), 5th (F♯), 6th (G♯)

Bmaj7sus4

Major 7th Suspended 4th

(1st position)

Chord Spelling

1st (B), 4th (E), 5th (F#), 7th (A#)

Bmaj7sus4
Major 7th Suspended 4th
(2nd position)

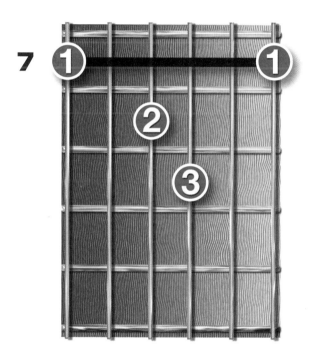

7

Chord Spelling
1st (B), 4th (E), 5th (F♯), 7th (A♯)

Bmaj9sus4

Major 9th Suspended 4th

(1st position)

Chord Spelling

1st (B), 4th (E), 5th (F#), 7th (A#)
9th (C#)

Bmaj9sus4
Major 9th Suspended 4th
(2nd position)

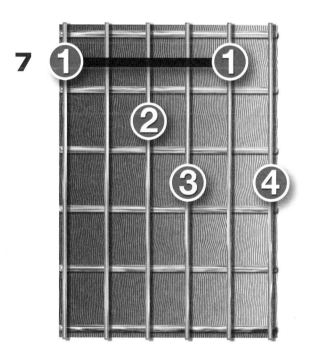

7

Chord Spelling

1st (B), 4th (E), 5th (F♯), 7th (A♯)
9th (C♯)

A
B♭/A♯
B
C
C♯/D♭
D
E♭/D♯
E
F
F♯/G♭
G
A♭/G♯
Other Chords

B9sus4

9th Suspended 4th

(1st position)

x

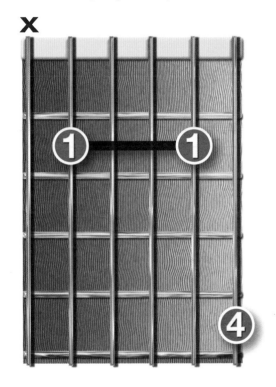

Chord Spelling

1st (B), 4th (E), 5th (F♯), ♭7th (A)
9th (C♯)

B9sus4

9th Suspended 4th

(2nd position)

A

Bb/A#

B

C

C#/Db

D

Eb/D#

E

F

F#/Gb

G

Ab/G#

Other Chords

7

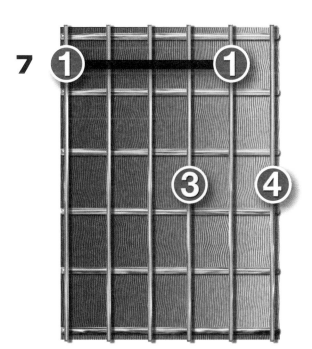

Chord Spelling

1st (B), 4th (E), 5th (F#), b7th (A)
9th (C#)

Csus2

Suspended 2nd

(1st position)

Chord Spelling

1st (C), 2nd (D), 5th (G)

A

B♭/A♯

B

C

C♯/D♭

D

E♭/D♯

E

F

F♯/G♭

G

A♭/G♯

Other Chords

Csus2

Suspended 2nd

(2nd position)

5

A
B♭/A♯
B
C
C♯/D♭
D
E♭/D♯
E
F
F♯/G♭
G
A♭/G♯
Other Chords

Chord Spelling

1st (C), 2nd (D), 5th (G)

A

B♭/A♯

B

C

C♯/D♭

D

E♭/D♯

E

F

F♯/G♭

G

A♭/G♯

Other
Chords

Cmaj11
Major 11th
(1st position)

Chord Spelling

1st (C), 3rd (E), 5th (G), 7th (B),
9th (D), 11th (F)

Cmaj11
Major 11th
(2nd position)

A
B♭/A♯
B
C
C♯/D♭
D
E♭/D♯
E
F
F♯/G♭
G
A♭/G♯
Other Chords

Chord Spelling

1st (C), 3rd (E), 5th (G), 7th (B),
9th (D), 11th (F)

Cm11
Minor 11th
(1st position)

Chord Spelling

1st (C), ♭3rd (E♭), 5th (G), ♭7th (B♭),
9th (D), 11th (F)

Cm11
Minor 11th

(2nd position)

A

B♭/A♯

B

C

C♯/D♭

D

E♭/D♯

E

F

F♯/G♭

G

A♭/G♯

Other Chords

6

Chord Spelling

1st (C), ♭3rd (E♭), 5th (G), ♭7th (B♭),
9th (D), 11th (F)

Cm maj11
Minor Major 11th
(1st position)

Chord Spelling

1st (C), ♭3rd (E♭), 5th (G), 7th (B)
9th (D), 11th (F)

Cm maj11
Minor Major 11th
(2nd position)

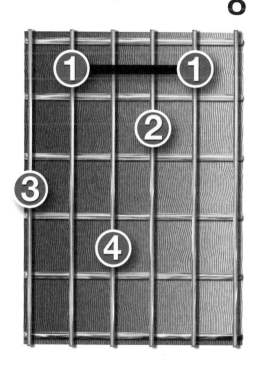

O

6

Chord Spelling

1st (C), ♭3rd (E♭), 5th (G), 7th (B)
9th (D), 11th (F)

♭/A♯

B

C

C♯/D♭

D

E♭/D♯

E

F

F♯/G♭

G

A♭/G♯

Other Chords

A

B♭/A♯

B

C

C♯/D♭

D

E♭/D♯

E

F

F♯/G♭

G

A♭/G♯

Other
Chords

Cmaj13

Major 13th

(1st position)

Chord Spelling

1st (C), 3rd (E), 5th (G), 7th (B)
9th (D), 11th (F), 13th (A)

Cmaj13
Major 13th
(2nd position)

A

B♭/A♯

B

C

C♯/D♭

D

E♭/D♯

E

F

F♯/G♭

G

A♭/G♯

Other Chords

7

Chord Spelling

1st (C), 3rd (E), 5th (G), 7th (B)
9th (D), 11th (F), 13th (A)

Cm13

Minor 13th

(1st position)

Chord Spelling

1st (C), ♭3rd (E♭), 5th (G), ♭7th (B♭)
9th (D), 11th (F), 13th (A)

A
B♭/A♯
B
C
C♯/D♭
D
E♭/D♯
E
F
F♯/G♭
G
A♭/G♯
Other Chords

Cm13

Minor 13th

(2nd position)

A

B♭/A♯

B

C

C♯/D♭

D

E♭/D♯

E

F

F♯/G♭

G

A♭/G♯

Other Chords

8

Chord Spelling

1st (C), ♭3rd (E♭), 5th (G), ♭7th (B♭)
9th (D), 11th (F), 13th (A)

A

B♭/A♯

B

C

C♯/D♭

D

E♭/D♯

E

F

F♯/G♭

G

A♭/G♯

Other Chords

Cm maj13
Minor Major 13th
(1st position)

Chord Spelling

1st (C), ♭3rd (E♭), 5th (G), 7th (B)
9th (D), 11th (F), 13th (A)

Cm maj13

Minor Major 13th

(2nd position)

A
Bb/A#
B
C
C#/Db
D
Eb/D#
E
F
F#/Gb
G
Ab/G#
Other Chords

Chord Spelling

1st (C), b3rd (Eb), 5th (G), 7th (B)
9th (D), 11th (F), 13th (A)

C+9

Major Add 9th

(1st position)

Chord Spelling

1st (C), 3rd (E), 5th (G), 9th (D)

C+9

Major Add 9th

(2nd position)

X

5

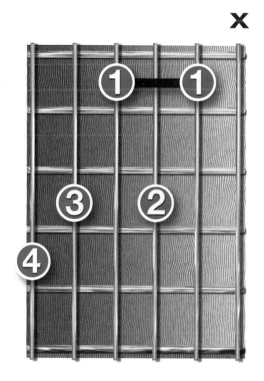

A

Bb/A#

B

C

C#/Db

D

Eb/D#

E

F

F#/Gb

G

Ab/G#

Other
Chords

Chord Spelling

1st (C), 3rd (E), 5th (G), 9th (D)

Cm+9

Minor Add 9th

(1st position)

Chord Spelling

1st (C), ♭3rd (E♭), 5th (G), 9th (D)

Cm+9

Minor Add 9th

(2nd position)

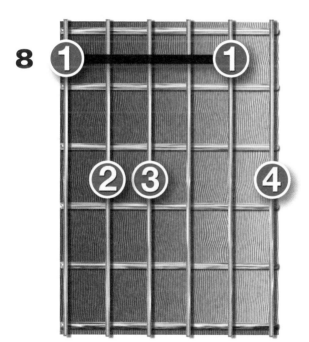

A

B♭/A#

B

C

C#/D♭

D

E♭/D#

E

F

F#/G♭

G

A♭/G#

Other Chords

8

Chord Spelling

1st (C), ♭3rd (E♭), 5th (G), 9th (D)

Cm6+9

Minor 6th Add 9th

(1st position)

Chord Spelling

1st (C), ♭3rd (E♭), 5th (G), 6th (A)
9th (D)

Cm6+9

Minor 6th Add 9th

(2nd position)

A

B♭/A♯

B

C

C♯/D♭

D

E♭/D♯

E

F

F♯/G♭

G

A♭/G♯

Other Chords

X

6

Chord Spelling

1st (C), ♭3rd (E♭), 5th (G), 6th (A)
9th (D)

C7+9

7th Add 9th

(1st position)

x

Chord Spelling

1st (C), 3rd (E), 5th (G), 7th (B♭)
9th (D)

C7+9

7th Add 9th

(2nd position)

5

Chord Spelling

1st (C), 3rd (E), 5th (G), 7th (B♭)
9th (D)

C6sus4

6th Suspended 4th

(1st position)

Chord Spelling

1st (C), 4th (F), 5th (G), 6th (A)

C6sus4
6th Suspended 4th
(2nd position)

X

3

Chord Spelling
1st (C), 4th (F), 5th (G), 6th (A)

A

B♭/A♯

B

C

C♯/D♭

D

E♭/D♯

E

F

F♯/G♭

G

A♭/G♯

Other Chords

Cmaj7sus4

Major 7th Suspended 4th

(1st position)

Chord Spelling

1st (C), 4th (F), 5th (G), 7th (B)

Cmaj7sus4
Major 7th Suspended 4th

(2nd position)

A
B♭/A#
B
C
C#/D♭
D
E♭/D#
E
F
F#/G♭
G
A♭/G#
Other Chords

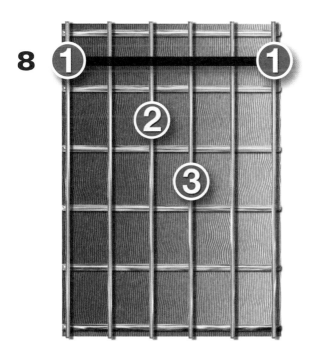

8

Chord Spelling

1st (C), 4th (F), 5th (G), 7th (B)

Cmaj9sus4

Major 9th Suspended 4th

(1st position)

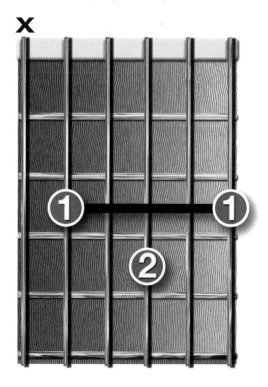

Chord Spelling

1st (C), 4th (F), 5th (G), 7th (B)
9th (D)

Cmaj9sus4
Major 9th Suspended 4th
(2nd position)

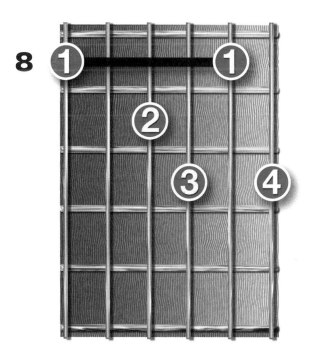

8

Chord Spelling

1st (C), 4th (F), 5th (G), 7th (B)
9th (D)

A

B♭/A#

B

C

C#/D♭

D

E♭/D#

E

F

F#/G♭

G

A♭/G#

Other
Chords

C9sus4

9th Suspended 4th

(1st position)

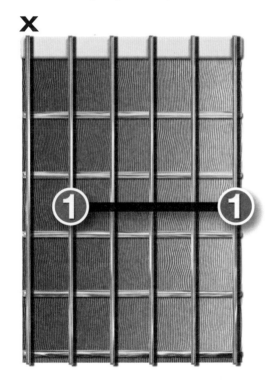

Chord Spelling

1st (C), 4th (F), 5th (G), ♭7th (B♭)
9th (D)

C9sus4

9th Suspended 4th

(2nd position)

A
B♭/A♯
B
C
C♯/D♭
D
E♭/D♯
E
F
F♯/G♭
G
A♭/G♯
Other Chords

8

Chord Spelling

1st (C), 4th (F), 5th (G), ♭7th (B♭)
9th (D)

A

Bb/A#

B

C

C#/Db

D

Eb/D#

E

F

F#/Gb

G

Ab/G#

Other
Chords

C#sus2

Suspended 2nd

(1st position)

Chord Spelling

1st (C#), 2nd (D#), 5th (G#)

C#sus2

Suspended 2nd

(2nd position)

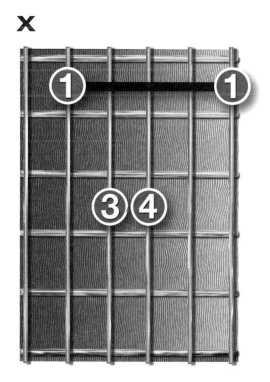

A

B♭/A#

B

C

C#/D♭

D

E♭/D#

E

F

F#/G♭

G

A♭/G#

Other
Chords

Chord Spelling

1st (C#), 2nd (D#), 5th (G#)

A

B♭/A♯

B

C

C♯/D♭

D

E♭/D♯

E

F

F♯/G♭

G

A♭/G♯

Other
Chords

C♯maj11

Major 11th

(1st position)

Chord Spelling

1st (C♯), 3rd (E♯), 5th (G♯), 7th (B♯),
9th (D♯), 11th (F♯)

C#maj11

Major 11th

(2nd position)

X X

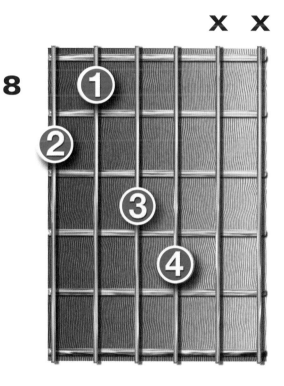

8

① ② ③ ④

Chord Spelling

1st (C#), 3rd (E#), 5th (G#), 7th (B#),
9th (D#), 11th (F#)

A
Bb/A#
B
C
C#/Db
D
Eb/D#
E
F
F#/Gb
G
Ab/G#
Other Chords

C#m11

Minor 11th

(1st position)

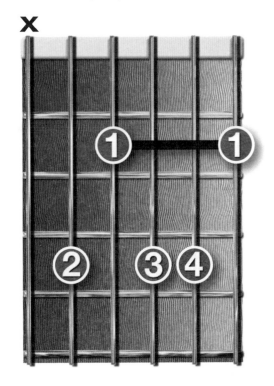

Chord Spelling

1st (C#), ♭3rd (E), 5th (G#), 7th (B#)
9th (D#), 11th (F#)

A
B♭/A#
B
C
C#/D♭
D
E♭/D#
E
F
F#/G♭
G
A♭/G#
Other Chords

C#m11

Minor 11th

(2nd position)

A

B♭/A#

B

C

C#/D♭

D

E♭/D#

E

F

F#/G♭

G

A♭/G#

Other Chords

7

Chord Spelling

1st (C#), ♭3rd (E), 5th (G#), 7th (B#)
9th (D#), 11th (F#)

A

B♭/A♯

B

C

C♯/D♭

D

E♭/D♯

E

F

F♯/G♭

G

A♭/G♯

Other Chords

C♯m maj11
Minor Major 11th
(1st position)

Chord Spelling
1st (C♯), ♭3rd (E), 5th (G♯), 7th (B♯)
9th (D♯), 11th (F♯)

C#m maj11

Minor Major 11th

(2nd position)

A

Bb/A#

B

C

C#/Db

D

Eb/D#

E

F

F#/Gb

G

Ab/G#

Other Chords

X

7

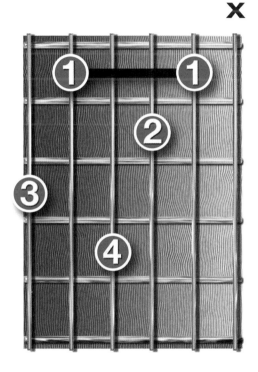

Chord Spelling

1st (C#), b3rd (E), 5th (G#), 7th (B#)
9th (D#), 11th (F#)

C#maj13

Major 13th

(1st position)

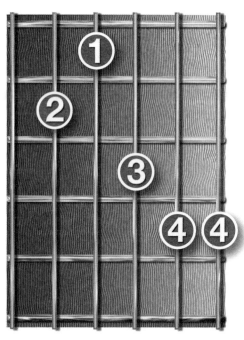

Chord Spelling

1st (C#), 3rd (E#), 5th (G#), 7th (B#)
9th (D#), 11th (F#), 13th (A#)

A

B♭/A#

B

C

C#/D♭

D

E♭/D#

E

F

F#/G♭

G

A♭/G#

Other Chords

C#maj13

Major 13th

(2nd position)

A

Bb/A#

B

C

C#/Db

D

Eb/D#

E

F

F#/Gb

G

Ab/G#

Other Chords

8

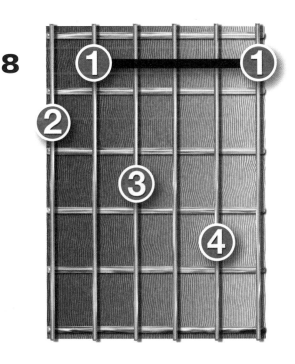

Chord Spelling

1st (C#), 3rd (E#), 5th (G#), 7th (B#)
9th (D#), 11th (F#), 13th (A#)

C#m13

Minor 13th

(1st position)

Chord Spelling

1st (C#), ♭3rd (E), 5th (G#), ♭7th (B)
9th (D#), 11th (F#), 13th (A#)

C#m13

Minor 13th

(2nd position)

A

B♭/A#

B

C

C#/D♭

D

E♭/D#

E

F

F#/G♭

G

A♭/G#

Other Chords

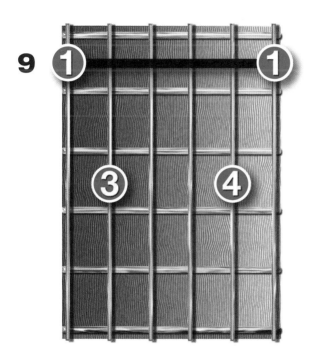

9

Chord Spelling

1st (C#), ♭3rd (E), 5th (G#), ♭7th (B)
9th (D#), 11th (F#), 13th (A#)

A

B♭/A♯

B

C

C♯/D♭

D

E♭/D♯

E

F

F♯/G♭

G

A♭/G♯

Other Chords

C♯m maj13

Minor Major 13th

(1st position)

x

4

Chord Spelling

1st (C♯), ♭3rd (E), 5th (G♯), 7th (B♯)
9th (D♯), 11th (F♯), 13th (A♯)

C#m maj13

Minor Major 13th

(2nd position)

A

B♭/A#

B

C

C#/D♭

D

E♭/D#

E

F

F#/G♭

G

A♭/G#

Other Chords

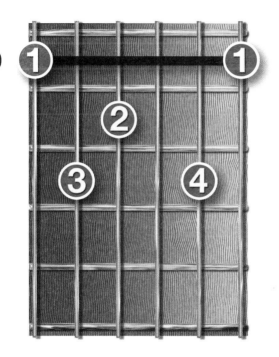

9

Chord Spelling

1st (C#), ♭3rd (E), 5th (G#), 7th (B#)
9th (D#), 11th (F#), 13th (A#)

C#+9

Major Add 9th

(1st position)

Chord Spelling

1st (C#), 3rd (E#), 5th (G#), 9th (D#)

C#+9

Major Add 9th

(2nd position)

X

6

A

Bb/A#

B

C

C#/Db

D

Eb/D#

E

F

F#/Gb

G

Ab/G#

Other Chords

Chord Spelling

1st (C#), 3rd (E#), 5th (G#), 9th (D#)

C#m+9

Minor Add 9th

(1st position)

Chord Spelling

1st (C#), ♭3rd (E), 5th (G#), 9th (D#)

C#m+9

Minor Add 9th

(2nd position)

A

B♭/A#

B

C

C#/D♭

D

E♭/D#

E

F

F#/G♭

G

A♭/G#

Other Chords

9

Chord Spelling

1st (C#), ♭3rd (E), 5th (G#), 9th (D#)

C#m6+9

Minor 6th Add 9th

(1st position)

A

B♭/A#

B

C

C#/D♭

D

E♭/D#

E

F

F#/G♭

G

A♭/G#

Other Chords

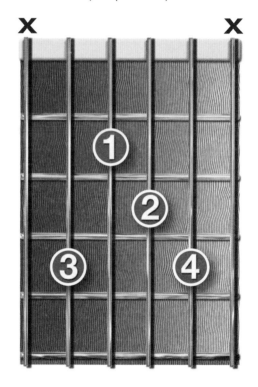

Chord Spelling

1st (C#), ♭3rd (E), 5th (G#), 6th (A#)
9th (D#)

C#m6+9

Minor 6th Add 9th

(2nd position)

X

7

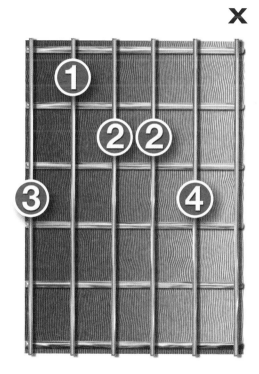

A

B♭/A#

B

C

C#/D♭

D

E♭/D#

E

F

F#/G♭

G

A♭/G#

Other Chords

Chord Spelling

1st (C#), ♭3rd (E), 5th (G#), 6th (A#)
9th (D#)

C#7+9

7th Add 9th

(1st position)

Chord Spelling

1st (C#), 3rd (E#), 5th (G#), 7th (B#)
9th (D#)

C#7+9

7th Add 9th

(2nd position)

6

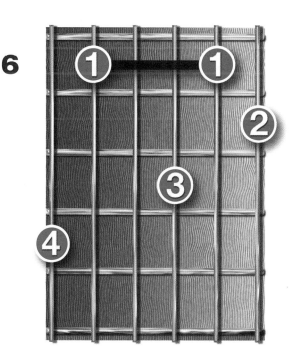

Chord Spelling

1st (C#), 3rd (E#), 5th (G#), 7th (B#)
9th (D#)

A
B♭/A#
B
C
C#/D♭
D
E♭/D#
E
F
F#/G♭
G
A♭/G#
Other Chords

C#6sus4

6th Suspended 4th

(1st position)

Chord Spelling
1st (C#), 4th (F#), 5th (G#), 6th (A#)

A
Bb/A#
B
C
C#/Db
D
Eb/D#
E
F
F#/Gb
G
Ab/G#
Other Chords

C♯6sus4

6th Suspended 4th

(2nd position)

A

B♭/A♯

B

C

C♯/D♭

D

E♭/D♯

E

F

F♯/G♭

G

A♭/G♯

Other Chords

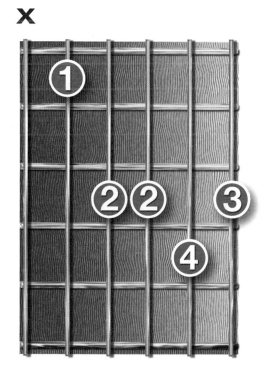

Chord Spelling

1st (C♯), 4th (F♯), 5th (G♯), 6th (A♯)

C#maj7sus4

Major 7th Suspended 4th

(1st position)

Chord Spelling

1st (C#), 4th (F#), 5th (G#), 7th (B#)

C#maj7sus4

Major 7th Suspended 4th

(2nd position)

A

B♭/A#

B

C

C#/D♭

D

E♭/D#

E

F

F#/G♭

G

A♭/G#

Other
Chords

X

4

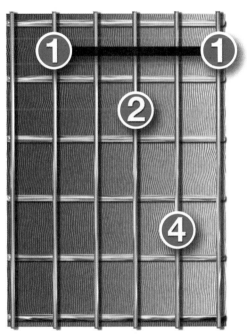

Chord Spelling

1st (C#), 4th (F#), 5th (G#), 7th (B#)

C#maj9sus4

Major 9th Suspended 4th

(1st position)

Chord Spelling

1st (C#), 4th (F#), 5th (G#), 7th (B#)
9th (D#)

C#maj9sus4

Major 9th Suspended 4th

(2nd position)

9

Chord Spelling

1st (C#), 4th (F#), 5th (G#), 7th (B#)
9th (D#)

A

B♭/A#

B

C

C#/D♭

D

E♭/D#

E

F

F#/G♭

G

A♭/G#

Other Chords

C#9sus4

9th Suspended 4th

(1st position)

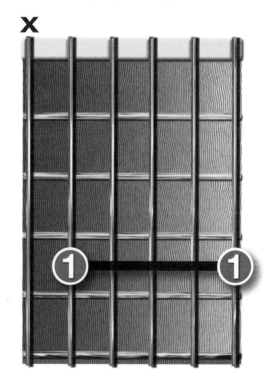

Chord Spelling

1st (C#), 4th (F#), 5th (G#), ♭7th (B)
9th (D#)

C#9sus4

9th Suspended 4th

(2nd position)

A

B♭/A#

B

C

C#/D♭

D

E♭/D#

E

F

F#/G♭

G

A♭/G#

Other Chords

X

4

Chord Spelling

1st (C#), 4th (F#), 5th (G#), ♭7th (B)
9th (D#)

Dsus2

Suspended 2nd

(1st position)

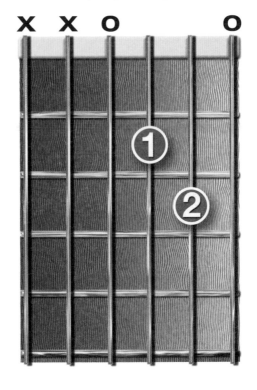

Chord Spelling

1st (D), 2nd (E), 5th (A)

Dsus2

Suspended 2nd

(2nd position)

X

5

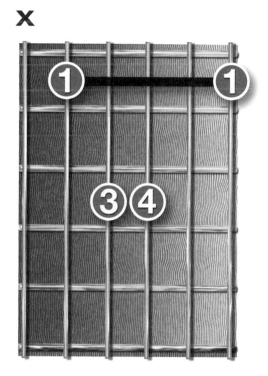

Chord Spelling

1st (D), 2nd (E), 5th (A)

A

B♭/A♯

B

C

C♯/D♭

D

E♭/D♯

E

F

F♯/G♭

G

A♭/G♯

Other
Chords

Dmaj11

Major 11th

(1st position)

Chord Spelling

1st (D), 3rd (F#), 5th (A), 7th (C#),
9th (E), 11th (G)

Dmaj11
Major 11th
(2nd position)

X

5

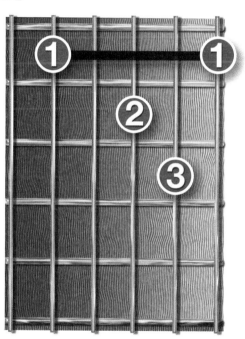

Chord Spelling

1st (D), 3rd (F♯), 5th (A), 7th (C♯),
9th (E), 11th (G)

A

B♭/A♯

B

C

C♯/D♭

D

E♭/D♯

E

F

F♯/G♭

G

A♭/G♯

Other
Chords

A
B♭/A#
B
C
C#/D♭
D
E♭/D#
E
F
F#/G♭
G
A♭/G#
Other
Chords

Dm11

Minor 11th

(1st position)

x

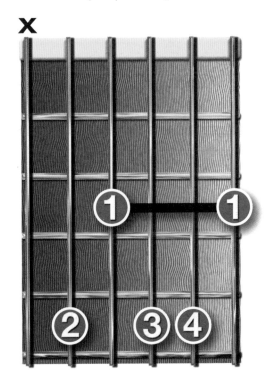

Chord Spelling

1st (D), ♭3rd (F), 5th (A), ♭7th (C),
9th (E), 11th (G)

Dm11

Minor 11th

(2nd position)

8

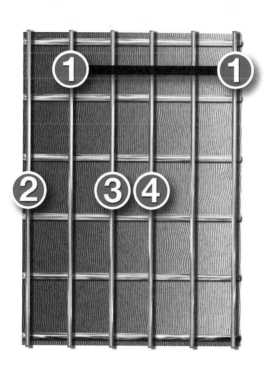

A

B♭/A♯

B

C

C♯/D♭

D

E♭/D♯

E

F

F♯/G♭

G

A♭/G♯

Other Chords

Chord Spelling

1st (D), ♭3rd (F), 5th (A), ♭7th (C),
9th (E), 11th (G)

Dm maj11
Minor Major 11th
(1st position)

X

Chord Spelling
1st (D), ♭3rd (F), 5th (A), 7th (C♯)
9th (E), 11th (G)

Dm maj11
Minor Major 11th
(2nd position)

X

8

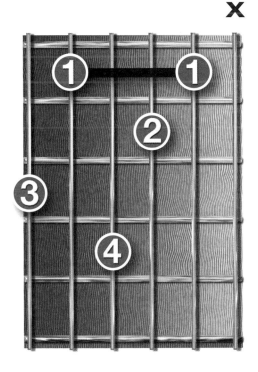

A
B♭/A♯
B
C
C♯/D♭
D
E♭/D♯
E
F
F♯/G♭
G
A♭/G♯
Other Chords

Chord Spelling
1st (D), ♭3rd (F), 5th (A), 7th (C♯)
9th (E), 11th (G)

Dmaj13

Major 13th

(1st position)

X

4

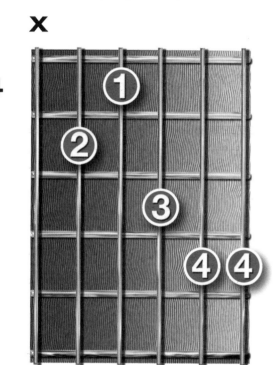

Chord Spelling

1st (D), 3rd (F♯), 5th (A), 7th (C♯)
9th (E), 11th (G), 13th (B)

A
B♭/A♯
B
C
C♯/D♭
D
E♭/D♯
E
F
F♯/G♭
G
A♭/G♯
Other Chords

Dmaj13
Major 13th

(2nd position)

9

Chord Spelling

1st (D), 3rd (F♯), 5th (A), 7th (C♯)
9th (E), 11th (G), 13th (B)

Dm13

Minor 13th

(1st position)

X

5

Chord Spelling

1st (D), ♭3rd (F), 5th (A), ♭7th (C)
9th (E), 11th (G), 13th (B)

Dm13

Minor 13th

(2nd position)

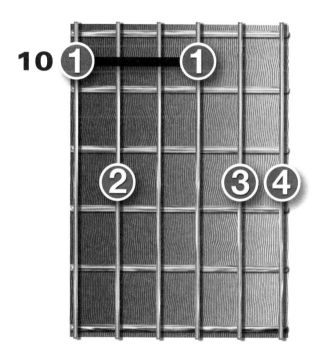

10

A

B♭/A#

B

C

C#/D♭

D

E♭/D#

E

F

F#/G♭

G

A♭/G#

Other Chords

Chord Spelling

1st (D), ♭3rd (F), 5th (A), ♭7th (C)
9th (E), 11th (G), 13th (B)

Dm maj13
Minor Major 13th
(1st position)

X

5

Chord Spelling
1st (D), ♭3rd (F), 5th (A), 7th (C♯)
9th (E), 11th (G), 13th (B)

A
B♭/A♯
B
C
C♯/D♭
D
E♭/D♯
E
F
F♯/G♭
G
A♭/G♯
Other Chords

Dm maj13
Minor Major 13th

(2nd position)

A

B♭/A♯

B

C

C♯/D♭

D

E♭/D♯

E

F

F♯/G♭

G

A♭/G♯

Other Chords

10

Chord Spelling

1st (D), ♭3rd (F), 5th (A), 7th (C♯)
9th (E), 11th (G), 13th (B)

D+9

Major Add 9th

(1st position)

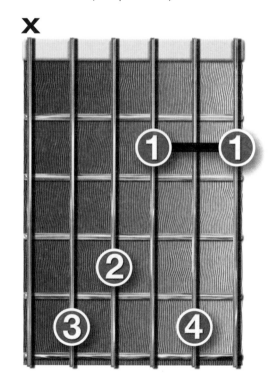

Chord Spelling

1st (D), 3rd (F♯), 5th (A), 9th (E)

D+9

Major Add 9th

(2nd position)

A

B♭/A♯

B

C

C♯/D♭

D

E♭/D♯

E

F

F♯/G♭

G

A♭/G♯

Other Chords

X

7

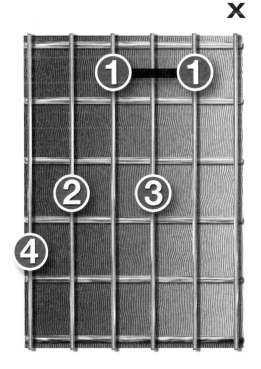

Chord Spelling

1st (D), 3rd (F♯), 5th (A), 9th (E)

Dm+9

Minor Add 9th

(1st position)

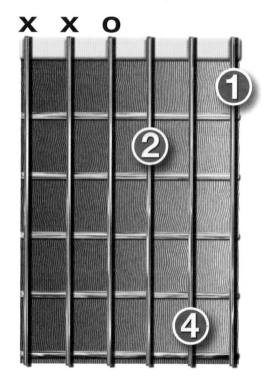

Chord Spelling

1st (D), ♭3rd (F), 5th (A), 9th (E)

Dm+9

Minor Add 9th

(2nd position)

A
Bb/A#
B
C
C#/Db
D
Eb/D#
E
F
F#/Gb
G
Ab/G#
Other Chords

X   O

5

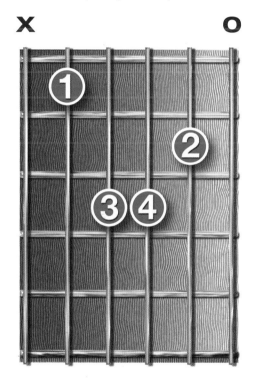

Chord Spelling

1st (D), b3rd (F), 5th (A), 9th (E)

Dm6+9

Minor 6th Add 9th

(1st position)

Chord Spelling

1st (D), ♭3rd (F), 5th (A), 6th (B)
9th (E)

A
B♭/A♯
B
C
C♯/D♭
D
E♭/D♯
E
F
F♯/G♭
G
A♭/G♯
Other Chords

Dm6+9

Minor 6th Add 9th

(2nd position)

X

8

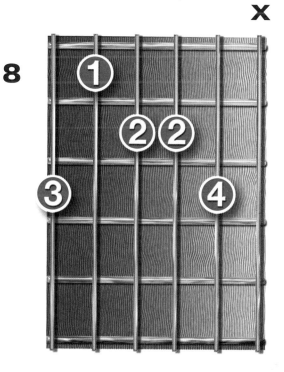

Chord Spelling

1st (D), ♭3rd (F), 5th (A), 6th (B)
9th (E)

A

B♭/A♯

B

C

C♯/D♭

D

E♭/D♯

E

F

F♯/G♭

G

A♭/G♯

Other
Chords

D7+9

7th Add 9th

(1st position)

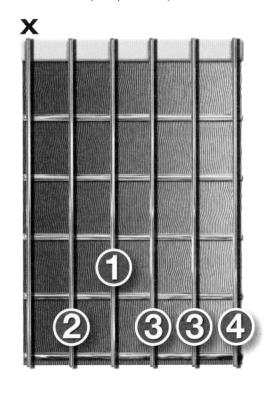

Chord Spelling

1st (D), 3rd (F♯), 5th (A), 7th (C♯)
9th (E)

D7+9

7th Add 9th

(2nd position)

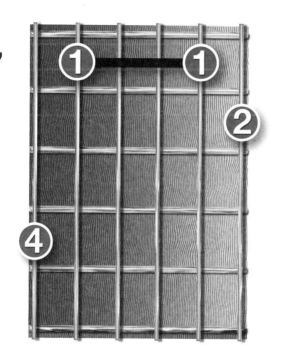

7

A

B♭/A♯

B

C

C♯/D♭

D

E♭/D♯

E

F

E♯/C♭

G

A♭/G♯

Other Chords

Chord Spelling

1st (D), 3rd (F♯), 5th (A), 7th (C♯)
9th (E)

D6sus4

6th Suspended 4th

(1st position)

Chord Spelling

1st (D), 4th (G), 5th (A), 6th (B)

D6sus4

6th Suspended 4th

(2nd position)

A
B♭/A♯
B
C
C♯/D♭
D
E♭/D♯
E
F
F♯/G♭
G
A♭/G♯
Other Chords

Chord Spelling

1st (D), 4th (G), 5th (A), 6th (B)

Dmaj7sus4

Major 7th Suspended 4th

(1st position)

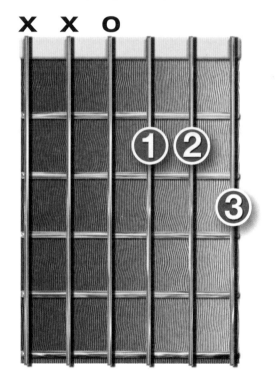

Chord Spelling

1st (D), 4th (G), 5th (A), 7th (C#)

Dmaj7sus4

Major 7th Suspended 4th

(2nd position)

X

5

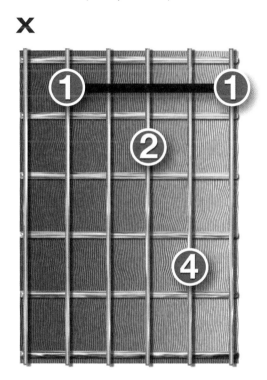

Chord Spelling

1st (D), 4th (G), 5th (A), 7th (C♯)

A

B♭/A♯

B

C

G♯/D♭

D

E♭/D♯

E

F

F♯/G♭

G

A♭/G♯

Other Chords

Dmaj9sus4

Major 9th Suspended 4th

(1st position)

X X O O O

③

Chord Spelling

1st (D), 4th (G), 5th (A), 7th (C#)
9th (E)

A
B♭/A#
B
C
C#/D♭
D
E♭/D#
E
F
F#/G♭
G
A♭/G#
Other Chords

Dmaj9sus4
Major 9th Suspended 4th

(2nd position)

A

B♭/A♯

B

C

C♯/D♭

D

E♭/D♯

E

F

F♯/G♭

G

A♭/G♯

Other Chords

X

5

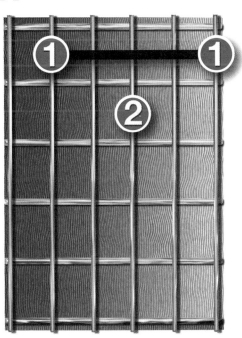

Chord Spelling

1st (D), 4th (G), 5th (A), 7th (C♯)
9th (E)

D9sus4

9th Suspended 4th

(1st position)

X X O O O

①

Chord Spelling

1st (D), 4th (G), 5th (A), ♭7th (C)
9th (E)

D9sus4

9th Suspended 4th

(2nd position)

X

5

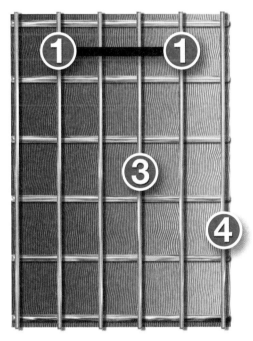

Chord Spelling

1st (D), 4th (G), 5th (A), ♭7th (C)
9th (E)

A
B♭/A♯
B
C
C♯/D♭
D
E♭/D♯
E
F
F♯/G♭
G
A♭/G♯
Other Chords

E♭sus2

Suspended 2nd

(1st position)

Chord Spelling

1st (E♭), 2nd (F), 5th (B♭)

E♭sus2

Suspended 2nd

(2nd position)

X

6

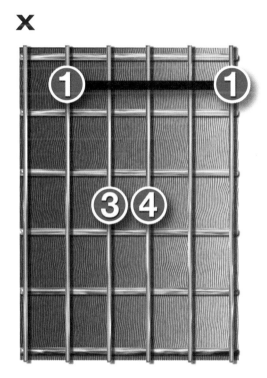

A

B♭/A#

B

C

C#/D♭

D

E♭/D#

E

F

F#/G♭

G

A♭/G#

Other Chords

Chord Spelling

1st (E♭), 2nd (F), 5th (B♭)

E♭maj11

Major 11th

(1st position)

x

3

Chord Spelling

1st (E♭), 3rd (G), 5th (B♭), 7th (D),
9th (F), 11th (A♭)

E♭maj11
Major 11th
(2nd position)

X

4

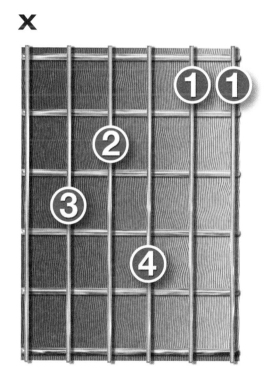

Chord Spelling

1st (E♭), 3rd (G), 5th (B♭), 7th (D),
9th (F), 11th (A♭)

A
B♭/A♯
B
C
C♯/D♭
D
E♭/D♯
E♯
F
F♯/G♭
G
A♭/G♯
Other Chords

E♭m11

Minor 11th

(1st position)

Chord Spelling

1st (E♭), ♭3rd (G♭), 5th (B♭), ♭7th (D♭),
9th (F), 11th (A♭)

E♭m11

Minor 11th

(2nd position)

9

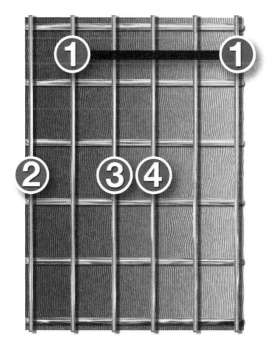

A

B♭/A#

B

C

C#/D♭

D

E♭/D#

E

F

F#/G♭

G

A♭/G#

Other Chords

Chord Spelling

1st (E♭), ♭3rd (G♭), 5th (B♭), ♭7th (D♭),
9th (F), 11th (A♭)

E♭m maj11

Minor Major 11th

(1st position)

4

Chord Spelling

1st (E♭), ♭3rd (G♭), 5th (B♭), 7th (D)
9th (F), 11th (A♭)

A

B♭/A#

B

C

C#/D♭

D

E♭/D#

E

F

F#/G♭

G

A♭/G#

Other
Chords

E♭m maj11
Minor Major 11th
(2nd position)

X

9

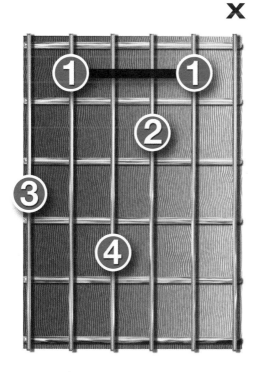

Chord Spelling

1st (E♭), ♭3rd (G♭), 5th (B♭), 7th (D)
9th (F), 11th (A♭)

A

B♭/A♯

B

C

C♯/D♭

D

E♭/D♯

E

F

F♯/G♭

G

A♭/G♯

Other Chords

E♭maj13

Major 13th

(1st position)

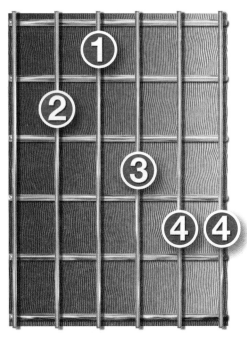

Chord Spelling

1st (E♭), 3rd (G), 5th (B♭), 7th (D)
9th (F), 11th (A♭), 13th (C)

A

B♭/A♯

B

C

C♯/D♭

D

E♭/D♯

E

F

F♯/G♭

G

A♭/G♯

Other Chords

E♭maj13
Major 13th
(2nd position)

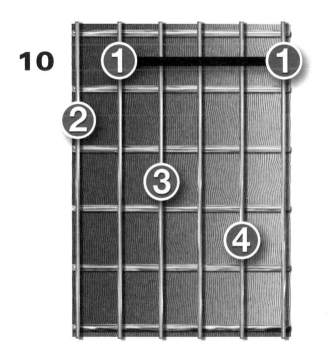

10

Chord Spelling

1st (E♭), 3rd (G), 5th (B♭), 7th (D)
9th (F), 11th (A♭), 13th (C)

E♭m13

Minor 13th

(1st position)

Chord Spelling

1st (E♭), ♭3rd (G♭), 5th (B♭), ♭7th (D♭)
9th (F), 11th (A♭), 13th (C)

E♭m13

Minor 13th

(2nd position)

A

B♭/A#

B

C

C#/D♭

D

E♭/D#

E

F

F#/G♭

G

A♭/G#

Other Chords

11

Chord Spelling

1st (E♭), ♭3rd (G♭), 5th (B♭), ♭7th (D♭)
9th (F), 11th (A♭), 13th (C)

A

B♭/A#

B

C

C#/D♭

D

E♭/D#

E

F

F#/G♭

G

A♭/G#

Other Chords

E♭m maj13

Minor Major 13th

(1st position)

X

6

Chord Spelling

1st (E♭), ♭3rd (G♭), 5th (B♭), 7th (D)
9th (F), 11th (A♭), 13th (C)

E♭m maj13

Minor Major 13th

(2nd position)

A

B♭/A♯

B

C

C♯/D♭

D

E♭/D♯

E

F

F♯/G♭

G

A♭/G♯

Other Chords

Chord Spelling

1st (E♭), ♭3rd (G♭), 5th (B♭), 7th (D)
9th (F), 11th (A♭), 13th (C)

E♭+9

Major Add 9th

(1st position)

X

3

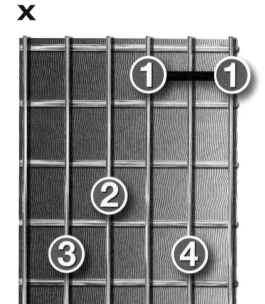

Chord Spelling

1st (E♭), 3rd (G), 5th (B♭), 9th (F)

E♭ +9

Major Add 9th

(2nd position)

A

B♭/A#

B

C

C#/D♭

D

E♭/D#

E

F

F#/G♭

G

A♭/G#

Other Chords

X

8

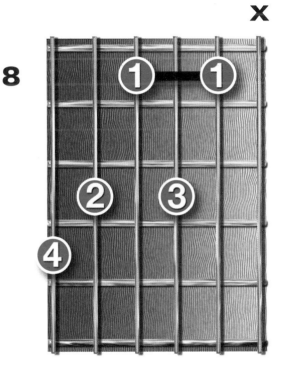

Chord Spelling

1st (E♭), 3rd (G), 5th (B♭), 9th (F)

E♭m+9

Minor Add 9th

(1st position)

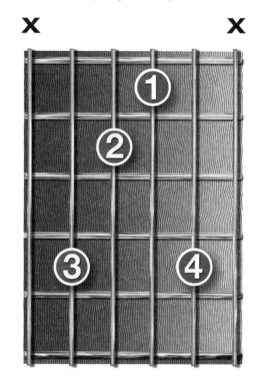

3

Chord Spelling

1st (E♭), ♭3rd (G♭), 5th (B♭), 9th (F)

E♭m+9

Minor Add 9th

(2nd position)

X X

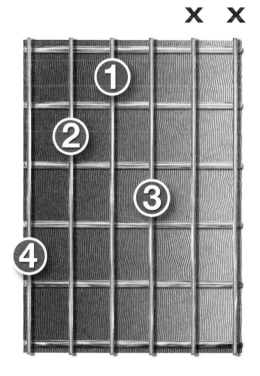

8

A

B♭/A♯

B

C

C♯/D♭

D

E♭/D♯

E

F

F♯/G♭

G

A♭/G♯

Other Chords

Chord Spelling

1st (E♭), ♭3rd (G♭), 5th (B♭), 9th (F)

E♭m6+9

Minor 6th Add 9th

(1st position)

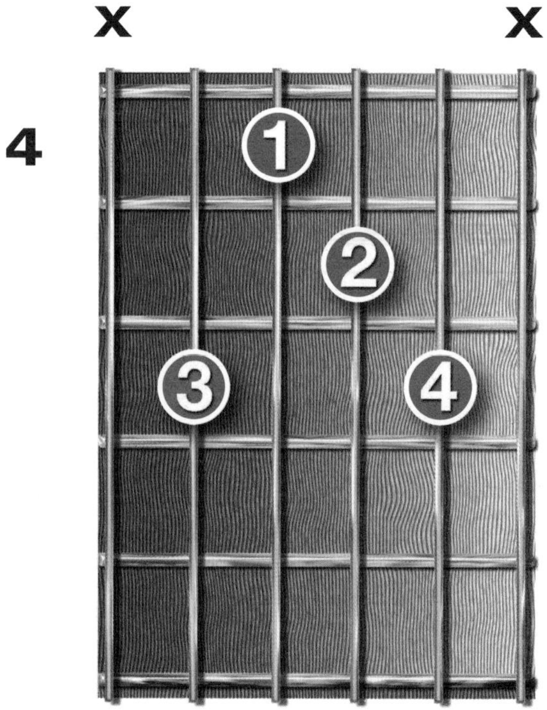

Chord Spelling

1st (E♭), ♭3rd (G♭), 5th (B♭), 6th (C)
9th (F)

E♭m6+9

Minor 6th Add 9th

(2nd position)

X

9

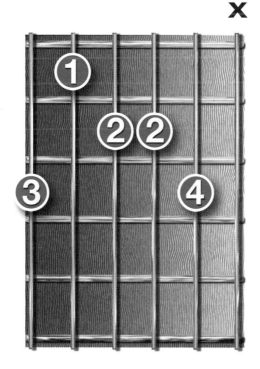

A

B♭/A♯

B

C

C♯/D♭

D

E♭/D♯

E

F

F♯/G♭

G

A♭/G♯

Other Chords

Chord Spelling

1st (E♭), ♭3rd (G♭), 5th (B♭), 6th (C)
9th (F)

E♭7+9

7th Add 9th

(1st position)

X

5

Chord Spelling

1st (E♭), 3rd (G), 5th (B♭), 7th (D)
9th (F)

E♭7+9

7th Add 9th

(2nd position)

8

A

B♭/A♯

B

C

C♯/D♭

D

E♭/D♯

E

F

F♯/G♭

G

A♭/G♯

Other Chords

Chord Spelling

1st (E♭), 3rd (G), 5th (B♭), 7th (D)
9th (F)

E♭6sus4

6th Suspended 4th

(1st position)

X X

Chord Spelling

1st (E♭), 4th (A♭), 5th (B♭), 6th (C)

E♭6sus4

6th Suspended 4th

(2nd position)

X

6

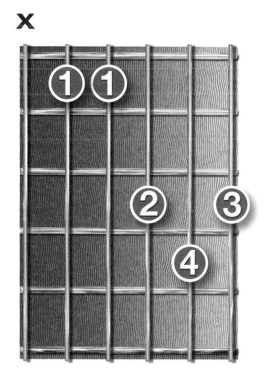

A

B♭/A#

B

C

C#/D♭

D

E♭/D#

E

F

F#/G♭

G

A♭/G#

Other Chords

Chord Spelling

1st (E♭), 4th (A♭), 5th (B♭), 6th (C)

E♭maj7sus4

Major 7th Suspended 4th

(1st position)

Chord Spelling

1st (E♭), 4th (A♭), 5th (B♭), 7th (D)

E♭maj7sus4

Major 7th Suspended 4th

(2nd position)

X

6

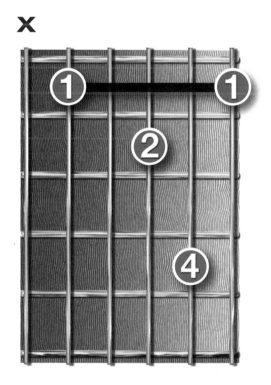

Chord Spelling

1st (E♭), 4th (A♭), 5th (B♭), 7th (D)

A

B♭/A#

B

C

C#/D♭

D

E♭/D#

E

F

F#/G♭

G

A♭/G#

Other Chords

A
B♭/A#
B
C
C#/D♭
D
E♭/D#
E
F
F#/G♭
G
A♭/G#
Other Chords

E♭maj9sus4

Major 9th Suspended 4th

(1st position)

Chord Spelling

1st (E♭), 4th (A♭), 5th (B♭), 7th (D)
9th (F)

E♭maj9sus4

Major 9th Suspended 4th

(2nd position)

A

B♭/A#

B

C

C#/D♭

D

E♭/D#

E

F

F#/G♭

G

A♭/G#

Other
Chords

X

6

Chord Spelling

1st (E♭), 4th (A♭), 5th (B♭), 7th (D)
9th (F)

E♭9sus4

9th Suspended 4th

(1st position)

x x

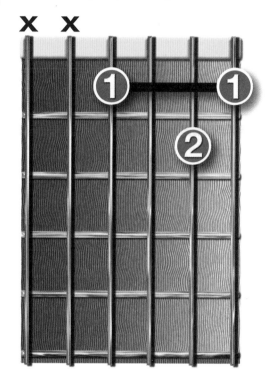

Chord Spelling

1st (E♭), 4th (A♭), 5th (B♭), ♭7th (D♭)
9th (F)

Eb9sus4

9th Suspended 4th

(2nd position)

A

Bb/A#

B

C

C#/Db

D

Eb/D#

E

F

F#/Gb

G

Ab/G#

Other
Chords

X

6

Chord Spelling

1st (Eb), 4th (Ab), 5th (Bb), b7th (Db)
9th (F)

Esus2

Suspended 2nd

(1st position)

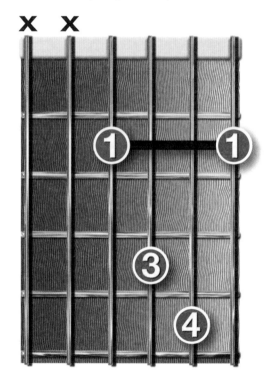

Chord Spelling

1st (E), 2nd (F#), 5th (B)

Esus2

Suspended 2nd

(2nd position)

A
B♭/A♯
B
C
C♯/D♭
D
E♭/D♯
E
F
F♯/G♭
G
A♭/G♯
Other Chords

Chord Spelling

1st (E), 2nd (F♯), 5th (B)

Emaj11

Major 11th

(1st position)

x

4

Chord Spelling

1st (E), 3rd (G#), 5th (B), 7th (D#),
9th (F#), 11th (A)

Emaj11
Major 11th
(2nd position)

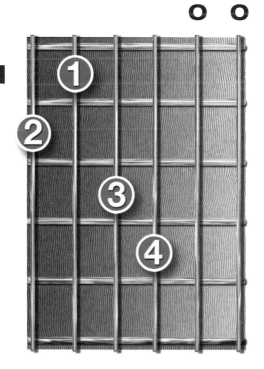

11

A

B♭/A♯

B

C

C♯/D♭

D

E♭/D♯

E

F

F♯/G♭

G

A♭/G♯

Other Chords

Chord Spelling

1st (E), 3rd (G♯), 5th (B), 7th (D♯), 9th (F♯), 11th (A)

Em11

Minor 11th

(1st position)

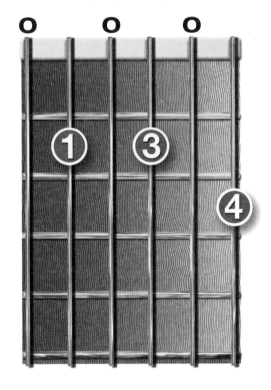

Chord Spelling

1st (E), ♭3rd (G), 5th (B), ♭7th (D),
9th (F♯), 11th (A)

Em11

Minor 11th

(2nd position)

A
B♭/A♯
B
C
C♯/D♭
D
E♭/D♯
E
F
F♯/G♭
G
A♭/G♯
Other Chords

X

5

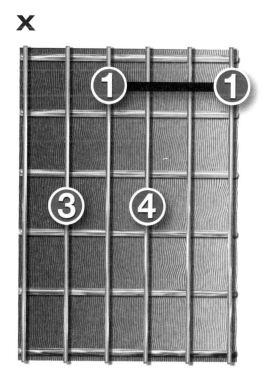

Chord Spelling

1st (E), ♭3rd (G), 5th (B), ♭7th (D),
9th (F♯), 11th (A)

Em maj11

Minor Major 11th

(1st position)

Chord Spelling

1st (E), ♭3rd (G), 5th (B), 7th (D♯)
9th (F♯), 11th (A)

A
B♭/A♯
B
C
C♯/D♭
D
E♭/D♯
E
F
F♯/G♭
G
A♭/G♯
Other Chords

Em maj11
Minor Major 11th
(2nd position)

X

5

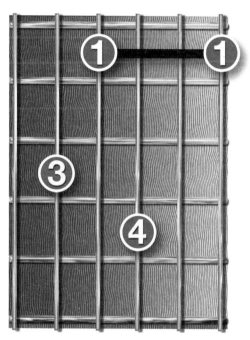

Chord Spelling
1st (E), ♭3rd (G), 5th (B), 7th (D♯)
9th (F♯), 11th (A)

A
B♭/A♯
B
C
C♯/D♭
D
E♭/D♯
E
F
F♯/G♭
G
A♭/G♯
Other Chords

Emaj13
Major 13th

(1st position)

Chord Spelling

1st (E), 3rd (G♯), 5th (B), 7th (D♯)
9th (F♯), 11th (A), 13th (C♯)

Emaj13

Major 13th

(2nd position)

X

6

A

B♭/A♯

B

C

C♯/D♭

D

E♭/D♯

E

F

F♯/G♭

G

A♭/G♯

Other
Chords

Chord Spelling

1st (E), 3rd (G♯), 5th (B), 7th (D♯)
9th (F♯), 11th (A), 13th (C♯)

Em13

Minor 13th

(1st position)

Chord Spelling

1st (E), ♭3rd (G), 5th (B), ♭7th (D)
9th (F♯), 11th (A), 13th (C♯)

A

B♭/A♯

B

C

C♯/D♭

D

E♭/D♯

E

F

F♯/G♭

G

A♭/G♯

Other Chords

Em13

Minor 13th

(2nd position)

X

7

Chord Spelling

1st (E), ♭3rd (G), 5th (B), ♭7th (D)
9th (F♯), 11th (A), 13th (C♯)

Em maj13
Minor Major 13th

(1st position)

Chord Spelling

1st (E), ♭3rd (G), 5th (B), 7th (D♯)
9th (F♯), 11th (A), 13th (C♯)

A
B♭/A♯
B
C
C♯/D♭
D
E♭/D♯
E
F
F♯/G♭
G
A♭/G♯
Other Chords

Em maj13
Minor Major 13th
(2nd position)

A
B♭/A♯
B
C
C♯/D♭
D
E♭/D♯
E
F
F♯/G♭
G
A♭/G♯
Other
Chords

x

7

Chord Spelling

1st (E), ♭3rd (G), 5th (B), 7th (D♯)
9th (F♯), 11th (A), 13th (C♯)

E+9

Major Add 9th

(1st position)

Chord Spelling

1st (E), 3rd (G♯), 5th (B), 9th (F♯)

E+9

Major Add 9th

(2nd position)

A
B♭/A♯
B
C
C♯/D♭
D
E♭/D♯
E
F
F♯/G♭
G
A♭/G♯
Other Chords

Chord Spelling

1st (E), 3rd (G♯), 5th (B), 9th (F♯)

Em+9

Minor Add 9th

(1st position)

Chord Spelling

1st (E), ♭3rd (G), 5th (B), 9th (F♯)

Em+9

Minor Add 9th

(2nd position)

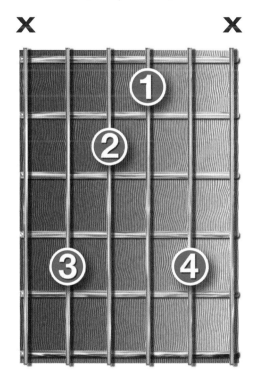

A
B♭/A♯
B
C
C♯/D♭
D
E♭/D♯
E
F
F♯/G♭
G
A♭/G♯
Other Chords

Chord Spelling

1st (E), ♭3rd (G), 5th (B), 9th (F♯)

Em6+9
Minor 6th Add 9th
(1st position)

Chord Spelling
1st (E), ♭3rd (G), 5th (B), 6th (C♯)
9th (F♯)

Em6+9

Minor 6th Add 9th

(2nd position)

A

B♭/A♯

B

C

C♯/D♭

D

E♭/D♯

E

F

F♯/G♭

G

A♭/G♯

Other Chords

X   X

5

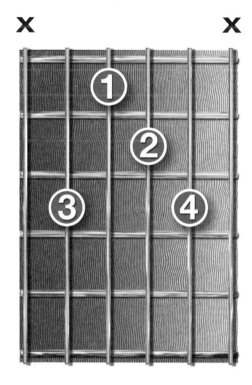

Chord Spelling

1st (E), ♭3rd (G), 5th (B), 6th (C♯)
9th (F♯)

A

B♭/A♯

B

C

C♯/D♭

D

E♭/D♯

E

F

F♯/G♭

G

A♭/G♯

Other
Chords

E7+9

7th Add 9th

(1st position)

Chord Spelling

1st (E), 3rd (G♯), 5th (B), 7th (D♯)
9th (F♯)

E7+9

7th Add 9th

(2nd position)

X

6

A

B♭/A♯

B

C

C♯/D♭

D

E♭/D♯

E

F

F♯/G♭

G

A♭/G♯

Other Chords

Chord Spelling

1st (E), 3rd (G♯), 5th (B), 7th (D♯)
9th (F♯)

E6sus4

6th Suspended 4th

(1st position)

Chord Spelling

1st (E), 4th (A), 5th (B), 6th (C♯)

E6sus4

6th Suspended 4th

(2nd position)

A

B♭/A♯

B

C

C♯/D♭

D

E♭/D♯

E

F

F♯/G♭

G

A♭/G♯

Other Chords

X

5

Chord Spelling

1st (E), 4th (A), 5th (B), 6th (C♯)

Emaj7sus4

Major 7th Suspended 4th

(1st position)

Chord Spelling

1st (E), 4th (A), 5th (B), 7th (D♯)

A

B♭/A♯

B

C

C♯/D♭

D

E♭/D♯

E

F

F♯/G♭

G

A♭/G♯

Other
Chords

Emaj7sus4

Major 7th Suspended 4th

(2nd position)

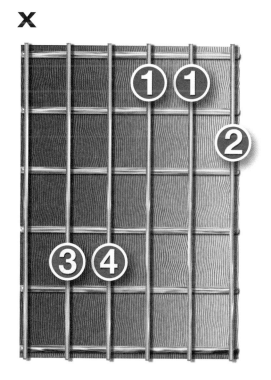

X

4

Chord Spelling

1st (E), 4th (A), 5th (B), 7th (D#)

A
Bb/A#
B
C
C#/Db
D
Eb/D#
E
F
F#/Gb
G
Ab/G#
Other Chords

Emaj9sus4

Major 9th Suspended 4th

(1st position)

Chord Spelling

1st (E), 4th (A), 5th (B), 7th (D♯)
9th (F♯)

A
B♭/A♯
B
C
C♯/D♭
D
E♭/D♯
E
F
F♯/G♭
G
A♭/G♯
Other Chords

Emaj9sus4
Major 9th Suspended 4th
(2nd position)

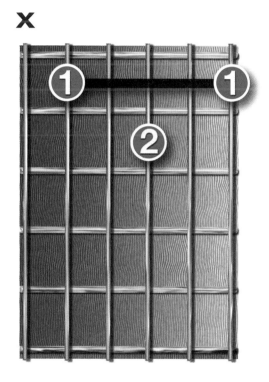

X

7

A
B♭/A♯
B
C
C♯/D♭
D
E♭/D♯
E
F
F♯/G♭
G
A♭/G♯
Other Chords

Chord Spelling

1st (E), 4th (A), 5th (B), 7th (D♯)
9th (F♯)

E9sus4

9th Suspended 4th

(1st position)

Chord Spelling

1st (E), 4th (A), 5th (B), ♭7th (D)
9th (F♯)

E9sus4

9th Suspended 4th

(2nd position)

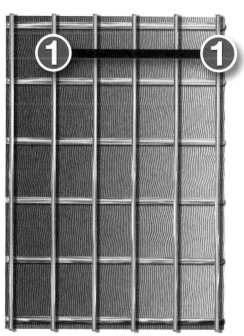

X

7

Chord Spelling

1st (E), 4th (A), 5th (B), ♭7th (D)
9th (F♯)

A
B♭/A♯
B
C
C♯/D♭
D
E♭/D♯
E
F
F♯/G♭
G
A♭/G♯
Other Chords

Fsus2

Suspended 2nd

(1st position)

Chord Spelling

1st (F), 2nd (G), 5th (C)

Fsus2

Suspended 2nd

(2nd position)

A

Bb/A#

B

C

C#/Db

D

Eb/D#

E

F

F#/Gb

G

Ab/G#

Other
Chords

X

8

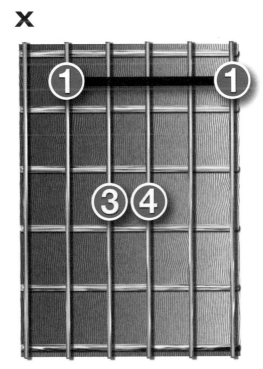

Chord Spelling

1st (F), 2nd (G), 5th (C)

A

B♭/A♯

B

C

C♯/D♭

D

E♭/D♯

E

F

F♯/G♭

G

A♭/G♯

Other
Chords

Fmaj11
Major 11th

(1st position)

Chord Spelling

1st (F), 3rd (A), 5th (C), 7th (E),
9th (G), 11th (B♭)

Fmaj11
Major 11th
(2nd position)

X

5

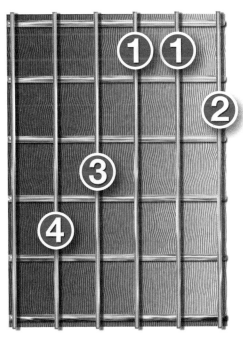

A

Bb/A#

B

C

C#/Db

D

Eb/D#

E

F

F#/Gb

G

Ab/G#

Other Chords

Chord Spelling

1st (F), 3rd (A), 5th (C), 7th (E),
9th (G), 11th (Bb)

A

B♭/A♯

B

C

C♯/D♭

D

E♭/D♯

E

F

F♯/G♭

G

A♭/G♯

Other
Chords

Fm11

Minor 11th

(1st position)

Chord Spelling

1st (F), ♭3rd (A♭), 5th (C), ♭7th (E♭),
9th (G), 11th (B♭)

Fm11

Minor 11th

(2nd position)

X

6

A

Bb/A#

B

C

C#/Db

D

Eb/D#

E

F

F#/Gb

G

Ab/G#

Other Chords

Chord Spelling

1st (F), b3rd (Ab), 5th (C), b7th (Eb), 9th (G), 11th (Bb)

Fm maj11

Minor Major 11th

(1st position)

X

5

Chord Spelling

1st (F), ♭3rd (A♭), 5th (C), 7th (E)
9th (G), 11th (B♭)

Fm maj11
Minor Major 11th
(2nd position)

X

6

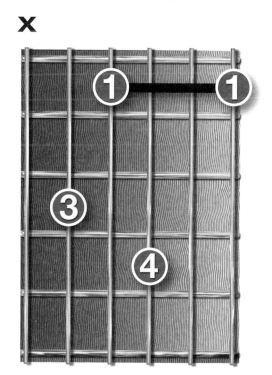

Chord Spelling

1st (F), ♭3rd (A♭), 5th (C), 7th (E)
9th (G), 11th (B♭)

A
B♭/A#
B
C
C#/D♭
D
E♭/D#
E
F
F#/G♭
G
A♭/G#
Other Chords

Fmaj13

Major 13th

(1st position)

Chord Spelling

1st (F), 3rd (A), 5th (C), 7th (E)
9th (G), 11th (Bb), 13th (D)

Fmaj13
Major 13th
(2nd position)

X

7

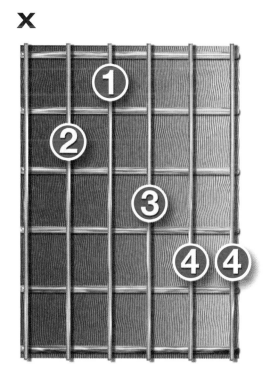

A

B♭/A♯

B

C

C♯/D♭

D

E♭/D♯

E

F

F♯/G♭

G

A♭/G♯

Other Chords

Chord Spelling

1st (F), 3rd (A), 5th (C), 7th (E)
9th (G), 11th (B♭), 13th (D)

Fm13

Minor 13th

(1st position)

A

B♭/A♯

B

C

C♯/D♭

D

E♭/D♯

E

F

F♯/G♭

G

A♭/G♯

Other
Chords

Chord Spelling

1st (F), ♭3rd (A♭), 5th (C), ♭7th (E♭)
9th (G), 11th (B♭), 13th (D)

Fm13
Minor 13th

(2nd position)

X

8

A

B♭/A♯

B

C

C♯/D♭

D

E♭/D♯

E

F

F♯/G♭

G

A♭/G♯

Other Chords

Chord Spelling

1st (F), ♭3rd (A♭), 5th (C), ♭7th (E♭)
9th (G), 11th (B♭), 13th (D)

Fm maj13
Minor Major 13th

(1st position)

Chord Spelling

1st (F), ♭3rd (A♭), 5th (C), 7th (E)
9th (G), 11th (B♭), 13th (D)

Fm maj13
Minor Major 13th
(2nd position)

X

8

A
B♭/A♯
B
C
C♯/D♭
D
E♭/D♯
E
F
F♯/G♭
G
A♭/G♯
Other Chords

Chord Spelling

1st (F), ♭3rd (A♭), 5th (C), 7th (E)
9th (G), 11th (B♭), 13th (D)

F+9

Major Add 9th

(1st position)

Chord Spelling

1st (F), 3rd (A), 5th (C), 9th (G)

F+9

Major Add 9th

(2nd position)

X

5

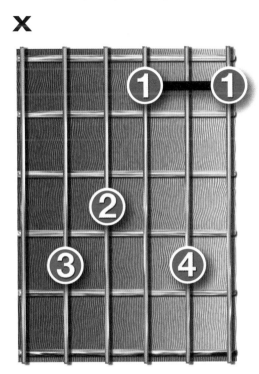

Chord Spelling

1st (F), 3rd (A), 5th (C), 9th (G)

A

B♭/A♯

B

C

C♯/D♭

D

E♭/D♯

E

F

F♯/G♭

G

A♭/G♯

Other Chords

A

B♭/A♯

B

C

C♯/D♭

D

E♭/D♯

E

F

F♯/G♭

G

A♭/G♯

Other Chords

Fm+9
Minor Add 9th

(1st position)

Chord Spelling

1st (F), ♭3rd (A♭), 5th (C), 9th (G)

Fm+9

Minor Add 9th

(2nd position)

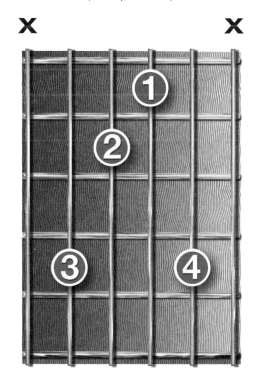

X   X

5

Chord Spelling

1st (F), ♭3rd (A♭), 5th (C), 9th (G)

A
B♭/A♯
B
C
C♯/D♭
D
E♭/D♯
E
F
F♯/G♭
G
A♭/G♯
Other Chords

Fm6+9
Minor 6th Add 9th

(1st position)

Chord Spelling

1st (F), ♭3rd (A♭), 5th (C), 6th (D)
9th (G)

Fm6+9

Minor 6th Add 9th

(2nd position)

X   X

5

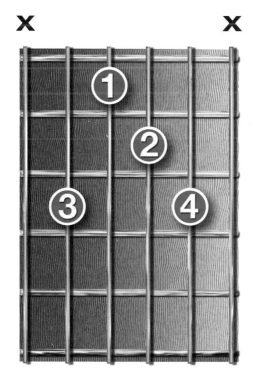

A

B♭/A#

B

C

C#/D♭

D

E♭/D#

E

F

F#/G♭

G

A♭/G#

Other
Chords

Chord Spelling

1st (F), ♭3rd (A♭), 5th (C), 6th (D)
9th (G)

F7+9

7th Add 9th

(1st position)

Chord Spelling

1st (F), 3rd (A), 5th (C), 7th (E)
9th (G)

A
B♭/A♯
B
C
C♯/D♭
D
E♭/D♯
E
F
F♯/G♭
G
A♭/G♯
Other Chords

F7+9

7th Add 9th

(2nd position)

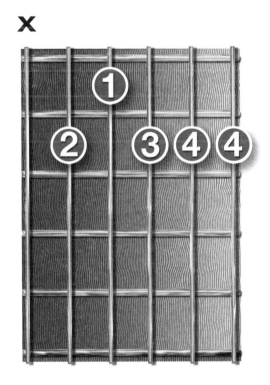

x

7

A

B♭/A♯

B

C

C♯/D♭

D

E♭/D♯

E

F

F♯/C♭

G

A♭/G♯

Other Chords

Chord Spelling

1st (F), 3rd (A), 5th (C), 7th (E)
9th (G)

F6sus4

6th Suspended 4th

(1st position)

Chord Spelling

1st (F), 4th (B♭), 5th (C), 6th (D)

F6sus4

6th Suspended 4th

(2nd position)

A

B♭/A♯

B

C

C♯/D♭

D

E♭/D♯

E

F

F♯/G♭

G

A♭/G♯

Other
Chords

X

8

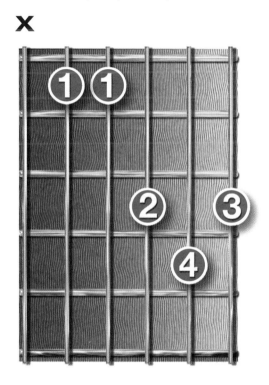

Chord Spelling

1st (F), 4th (B♭), 5th (C), 6th (D)

Fmaj7sus4
Major 7th Suspended 4th
(1st position)

Chord Spelling
1st (F), 4th (B♭), 5th (C), 7th (E)

A
B♭/A♯
B
C
C♯/D♭
D
E♭/D♯
E
F
F♯/G♭
G
A♭/G♯
Other Chords

Fmaj7sus4

Major 7th Suspended 4th

(2nd position)

X X

3

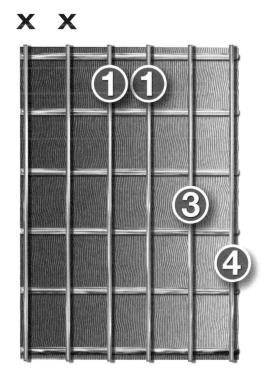

Chord Spelling

1st (F), 4th (B♭), 5th (C), 7th (E)

A
B♭/A#
B
C
C#/D♭
D
E♭/D#
E
F
F#/G♭
G
A♭/G#
Other Chords

A
B♭/A#
B
C
C#/D♭
D
E♭/D#
E
F
F#/G♭
G
A♭/G#
Other Chords

Fmaj9sus4

Major 9th Suspended 4th

(1st position)

Chord Spelling

1st (F), 4th (B♭), 5th (C), 7th (E)
9th (G)

Fmaj9sus4

Major 9th Suspended 4th

(2nd position)

X

8

Chord Spelling

1st (F), 4th (B♭), 5th (C), 7th (E)
9th (G)

A

B♭/A♯

B

C

C♯/D♭

D

E♭/D♯

E

F

F♯/G♭

G

A♭/G♯

Other Chords

F9sus4

9th Suspended 4th

(1st position)

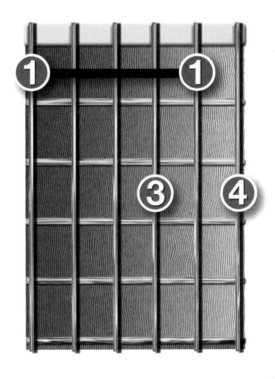

Chord Spelling

1st (F), 4th (B♭), 5th (C), ♭7th (E♭)
9th (G)

F9sus4

9th Suspended 4th

(2nd position)

X

8

A

B♭/A♯

B

C

C♯/D♭

D

E♭/D♯

E

F

F♯/G♭

G

A♭/G♯

Other Chords

Chord Spelling

1st (F), 4th (B♭), 5th (C), ♭7th (E♭)
9th (G)

F#sus2

Suspended 2nd

(1st position)

A
Bb/A#
B
C
C#/Db
D
Eb/D#
E
F
F#/Gb
G
Ab/G#
Other Chords

Chord Spelling

1st (F#), 2nd (G#), 5th (C#)

F#sus2

Suspended 2nd

(2nd position)

A

B♭/A#

B

C

C#/D♭

D

E♭/D#

E

F

F#/G♭

G

A♭/G#

Other Chords

Chord Spelling

1st (F#), 2nd (G#), 5th (C#)

F#maj11
Major 11th
(1st position)

O X

Chord Spelling

1st (F#), 3rd (A#), 5th (C#), 7th (E#),
9th (G#), 11th (B)

F#maj11

Major 11th

(2nd position)

A
B♭/A#
B
C
C#/D♭
D
E♭/D#
E
F
F#/G♭
G
A♭/G#
Other Chords

X

6

Chord Spelling

1st (F#), 3rd (A#), 5th (C#), 7th (E#), 9th (G#), 11th (B)

F#m11

Minor 11th

(1st position)

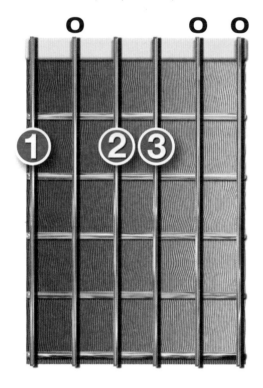

Chord Spelling

1st (F#), ♭3rd (A), 5th (C#), ♭7th (E),
9th (G#), 11th (B)

A

B♭/A#

B

C

C#/D♭

D

E♭/D#

E

F

F#/G♭

G

A♭/G#

Other Chords

F#m11

Minor 11th

(2nd position)

7

Chord Spelling

1st (F#), b3rd (A), 5th (C#), b7th (E),
9th (G#), 11th (B)

A

Bb/A#

B

C

C#/Db

D

Eb/D#

E

F

F#/Gb

G

Ab/G#

Other
Chords

A

B♭/A♯

B

C

C♯/D♭

D

E♭/D♯

E

F

F♯/G♭

G

A♭/G♯

Other
Chords

F♯m maj11
Minor Major 11th

(1st position)

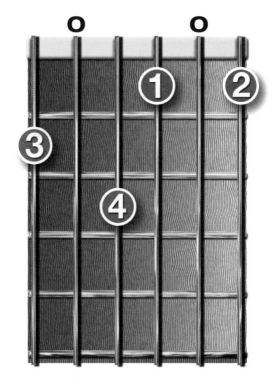

Chord Spelling

1st (F♯), ♭3rd (A), 5th (C♯), 7th (E♯)
9th (G♯), 11th (B)

F#m maj11
Minor Major 11th
(2nd position)

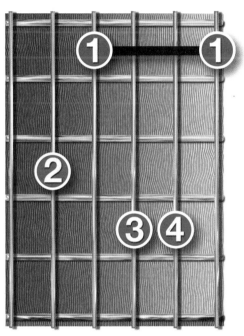

A
B♭/A#
B
C
C#/D♭
D
E♭/D#
E
F
F#/G♭
G
A♭/G#
Other Chords

Chord Spelling

1st (F#), ♭3rd (A), 5th (C#), 7th (E#)
9th (G#), 11th (B)

F#maj13

Major 13th

(1st position)

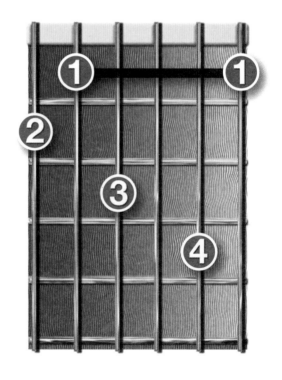

Chord Spelling

1st (F#), 3rd (A#), 5th (C#), 7th (E#)
9th (G#), 11th (B), 13th (D#)

A
B♭/A#
B
C
C#/D♭
D
E♭/D#
E
F
F#/G♭
G
A♭/G#
Other Chords

F#maj13

Major 13th

(2nd position)

X

8

Chord Spelling

1st (F#), 3rd (A#), 5th (C#), 7th (E#)
9th (G#), 11th (B), 13th (D#)

A

B♭/A#

B

C

C#/D♭

D

E♭/D#

E

F

F#/G♭

G

A♭/G#

Other
Chords

F#m13

Minor 13th

(1st position)

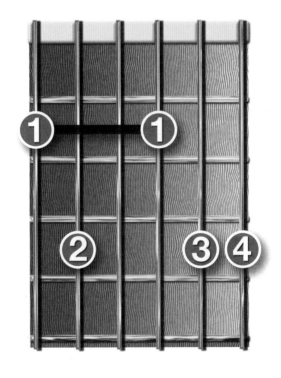

Chord Spelling

1st (F#), ♭3rd (A), 5th (C#), ♭7th (E)
9th (G#), 11th (B), 13th (D#)

A

B♭/A#

B

C

C#/D♭

D

E♭/D#

E

F

F#/G♭

G

A♭/G#

Other
Chords

F#m13

Minor 13th

(2nd position)

X

9

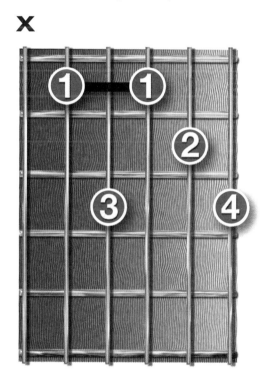

A

B♭/A#

B

C

C#/D♭

D

E♭/D#

E

F

F#/G♭

G

A♭/G#

Other Chords

Chord Spelling

1st (F#), ♭3rd (A), 5th (C#), ♭7th (E)
9th (G#), 11th (B), 13th (D#)

F#m maj13

Minor Major 13th

(1st position)

Chord Spelling

1st (F#), ♭3rd (A), 5th (C#), 7th (E#)
9th (G#), 11th (B), 13th (D#)

F#m maj13

Minor Major 13th

(2nd position)

X

9

A

Bb/A#

B

C

C#/Db

D

Eb/D#

E

F

F#/Gb

G

Ab/G#

Other
Chords

Chord Spelling

1st (F#), b3rd (A), 5th (C#), 7th (E#)
9th (G#), 11th (B), 13th (D#)

F#+9

Major Add 9th

(1st position)

A
B♭/A#
B
C
C#/D♭
D
E♭/D#
E
F
F#/G♭
G
A♭/G#
Other Chords

X X

① ② ③ ④

Chord Spelling

1st (F#), 3rd (A#), 5th (C#), 9th (G#)

F♯+9

Major Add 9th

(2nd position)

A

B♭/A♯

B

C

C♯/D♭

D

E♭/D♯

E

F

F♯/G♭

G

A♭/G♯

Other Chords

X

6

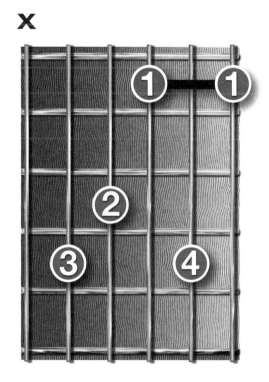

Chord Spelling

1st (F♯), 3rd (A♯), 5th (C♯), 9th (G♯)

A
B♭/A♯
B
C
C♯/D♭
D
E♭/D♯
E
F
F♯/G♭
G
A♭/G♯
Other
Chords

F♯m+9

Minor Add 9th

(1st position)

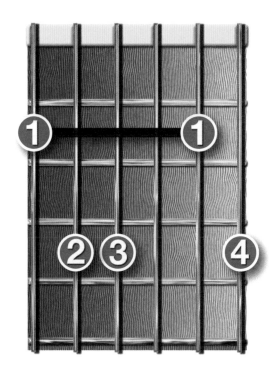

Chord Spelling

1st (F♯), ♭3rd (A), 5th (C♯), 9th (G♯)

F#m+9

Minor Add 9th

(2nd position)

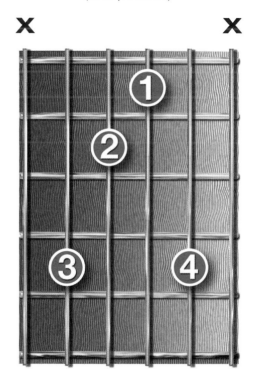

X   **X**

6

A
Bb/A#
B
C
C#/Db
D
Eb/D#
E
F
F#/Gb
G
Ab/G#
Other Chords

Chord Spelling

1st (F#), b3rd (A), 5th (C#), 9th (G#)

F#m6+9

Minor 6th Add 9th

(1st position)

Chord Spelling

1st (F#), ♭3rd (A), 5th (C#), 6th (D#)
9th (G#)

F#m6+9

Minor 6th Add 9th

(2nd position)

A

B♭/A#

B

C

C#/D♭

D

E♭/D#

E

F

F#/G♭

G

A♭/G#

Other Chords

X   X

7

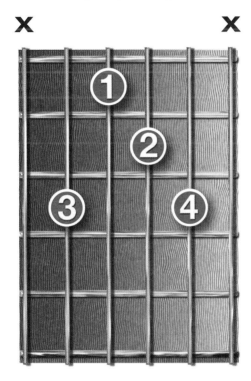

Chord Spelling

1st (F#), ♭3rd (A), 5th (C#), 6th (D#)
9th (G#)

F#7+9

7th Add 9th

(1st position)

A
Bb/A#
B
C
C#/Db
D
Eb/D#
E
F
F#/Gb
G
Ab/G#
Other Chords

Chord Spelling

1st (F#), 3rd (A#), 5th (C#), 7th (E#)
9th (G#)

F#7+9

7th Add 9th

(2nd position)

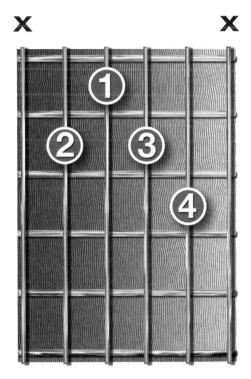

X   X

8

A

B♭/A#

B

C

C#/D♭

D

E♭/D#

E

F

F#/G♭

G

A♭/G#

Other
Chords

Chord Spelling

1st (F#), 3rd (A#), 5th (C#), 7th (E#)
9th (G#)

F♯6sus4

6th Suspended 4th

(1st position)

Chord Spelling

1st (F♯), 4th (B), 5th (C♯), 6th (D♯)

F#6sus4

6th Suspended 4th

(2nd position)

A
Bb/A#
B
C
C#/Db
D
Eb/D#
E
F
F#/Gb
G
Ab/G#
Other
Chords

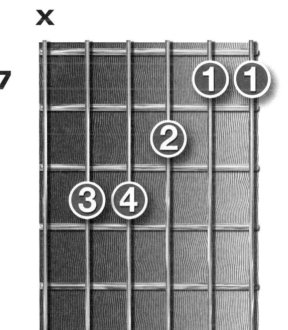

Chord Spelling

1st (F#), 4th (B), 5th (C#), 6th (D#)

A
B♭/A#
B
C
C#/D♭
D
E♭/D#
E
F
F#/G♭
G
A♭/G#
Other Chords

F#maj7sus4

Major 7th Suspended 4th

(1st position)

Chord Spelling

1st (F#), 4th (B), 5th (C#), 7th (E#)

F#maj7sus4

Major 7th Suspended 4th

(2nd position)

A
B♭/A#
B
C
C#/D♭
D
E♭/D#
E
F
F#/G♭
G
A♭/G#
Other Chords

X

6

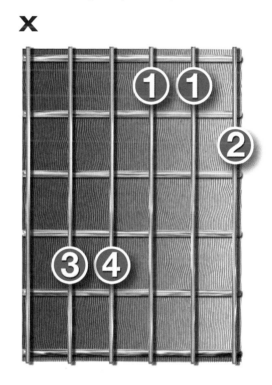

Chord Spelling

1st (F#), 4th (B), 5th (C#), 7th (E#)

F#maj9sus4
Major 9th Suspended 4th
(1st position)

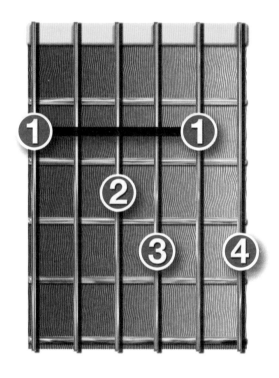

A
B♭/A#
B
C
C#/D♭
D
E♭/D#
E
F
F#/G♭
G
A♭/G#
Other Chords

Chord Spelling
1st (F#), 4th (B), 5th (C#), 7th (E#)
9th (G#)

F#maj9sus4
Major 9th Suspended 4th
(2nd position)

X

9

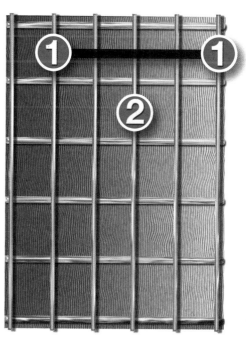

Chord Spelling

1st (F#), 4th (B), 5th (C#), 7th (E#)
9th (G#)

F#9sus4

9th Suspended 4th

(1st position)

Chord Spelling

1st (F#), 4th (B), 5th (C#), ♭7th (E)
9th (G#)

F♯9sus4

9th Suspended 4th

(2nd position)

X

9

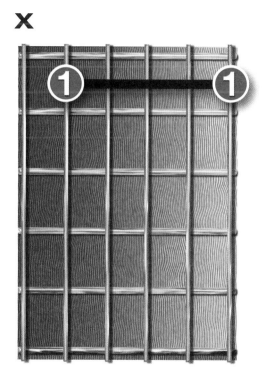

Chord Spelling

1st (F♯), 4th (B), 5th (C♯), ♭7th (E)
9th (G♯)

A

B♭/A♯

B

C

C♯/D♭

D

E♭/D♯

E

F

F♯/G♭

G

A♭/G♯

Other
Chords

Gsus2

Suspended 2nd

(1st position)

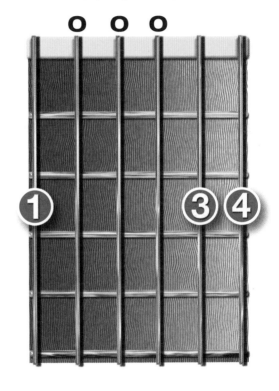

Chord Spelling

1st (G), 2nd (A), 5th (D)

Gsus2

Suspended 2nd

(2nd position)

A

B♭/A♯

B

C

C♯/D♭

D

E♭/D♯

E

F

F♯/G♭

G

A♭/G♯

Other Chords

X X

5

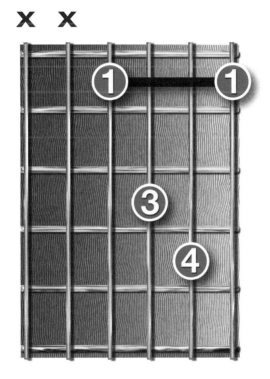

Chord Spelling

1st (G), 2nd (A), 5th (D)

Gmaj11

Major 11th

(1st position)

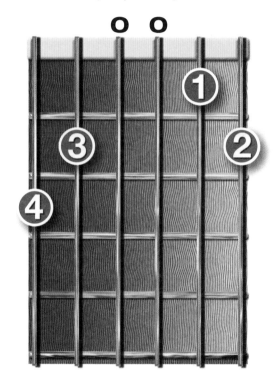

Chord Spelling

1st (G), 3rd (B), 5th (D), 7th (F#),
9th (A), 11th (C)

Gmaj11
Major 11th
(2nd position)

X

7

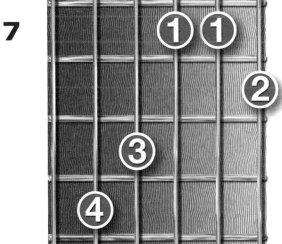

A
B♭/A♯
B
C
C♯/D♭
D
E♭/D♯
E
F
F♯/G♭
G
A♭/G♯
Other Chords

Chord Spelling

1st (G), 3rd (B), 5th (D), 7th (F♯), 9th (A), 11th (C)

Gm11
Minor 11th
(1st position)

Chord Spelling

1st (G), ♭3rd (B♭), 5th (D), ♭7th (F),
9th (A), 11th (C)

A

B♭/A♯

B

C

C♯/D♭

D

E♭/D♯

E

F

F♯/G♭

G

A♭/G♯

Other
Chords

Gm11

Minor 11th

(2nd position)

3

A

Bb/A#

B

C

C#/Db

D

Eb/D#

E

F

F#/Gb

G

Ab/G#

Other Chords

Chord Spelling

1st (G), b3rd (Bb), 5th (D), b7th (F),
9th (A), 11th (C)

A
B♭/A♯
B
C
C♯/D♭
D
E♭/D♯
E
F
F♯/G♭
G
A♭/G♯
Other Chords

Gm maj11

Minor Major 11th

(1st position)

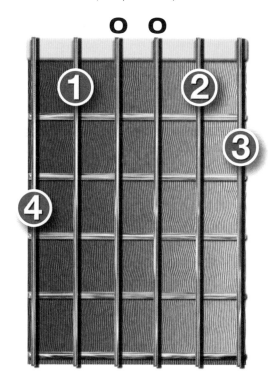

Chord Spelling

1st (G), ♭3rd (B♭), 5th (D), 7th (F♯)
9th (A), 11th (C)

Gm maj11
Minor Major 11th

(2nd position)

X

8

Chord Spelling

1st (G), ♭3rd (B♭), 5th (D), 7th (F♯)
9th (A), 11th (C)

A

B♭/A♯

B

C

C♯/D♭

D

E♭/D♯

E

F

F♯/G♭

G

A♭/G♯

Other Chords

A

B♭/A♯

B

C

C♯/D♭

D

E♭/D♯

E

F

F♯/G♭

G

A♭/G♯

Other Chords

Gmaj13
Major 13th

(1st position)

Chord Spelling

1st (G), 3rd (B), 5th (D), 7th (F♯)
9th (A), 11th (C), 13th (E)

Gmaj13
Major 13th

(2nd position)

A

B♭/A♯

B

C

C♯/D♭

D

E♭/D♯

E

F

F♯/G♭

G

A♭/G♯

Other Chords

X

9

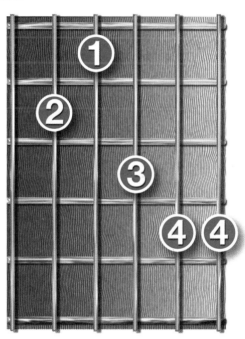

Chord Spelling

1st (G), 3rd (B), 5th (D), 7th (F♯)
9th (A), 11th (C), 13th (E)

Gm13

Minor 13th

(1st position)

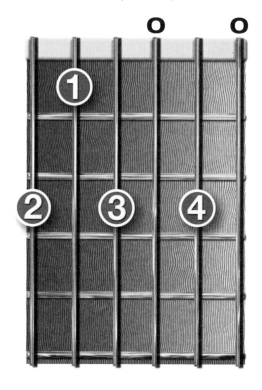

Chord Spelling

1st (G), ♭3rd (B♭), 5th (D), ♭7th (F)
9th (A), 11th (C), 13th (E)

Gm13

Minor 13th

(2nd position)

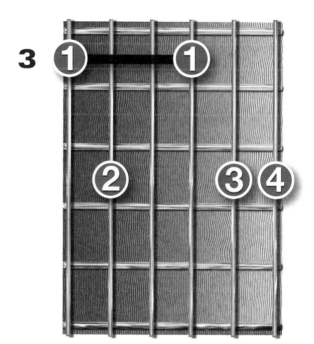

A
B♭/A♯
B
C
C♯/D♭
D
E♭/D♯
E
F
F♯/G♭
G
A♭/G♯
Other Chords

3

Chord Spelling

1st (G), ♭3rd (B♭), 5th (D), ♭7th (F)
9th (A), 11th (C), 13th (E)

A
Bb/A#
B
C
C#/Db
D
Eb/D#
E
F
F#/Gb
G
Ab/G#
Other
Chords

Gm maj13
Minor Major 13th

(1st position)

Chord Spelling

1st (G), b3rd (Bb), 5th (D), 7th (F#)
9th (A), 11th (C), 13th (E)

Gm maj13
Minor Major 13th
(2nd position)

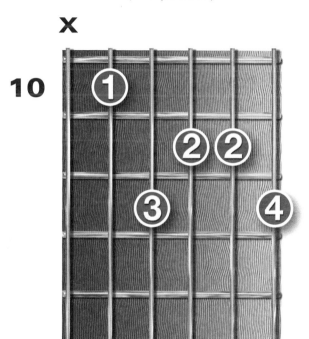

X

10

A
B♭/A♯
B
C
C♯/D♭
D
E♭/D♯
E
F
F♯/G♭
G
A♭/G♯
Other Chords

Chord Spelling

1st (G), ♭3rd (B♭), 5th (D), 7th (F♯)
9th (A), 11th (C), 13th (E)

G+9

Major Add 9th

(1st position)

Chord Spelling

1st (G), 3rd (B), 5th (D), 9th (A)

A

B♭/A♯

B

C

C♯/D♭

D

E♭/D♯

E

F

F♯/G♭

G

A♭/G♯

Other Chords

G+9

Major Add 9th

(2nd position)

A
B♭/A♯
B
C
C♯/D♭
D
E♭/D♯
E
F
F♯/G♭
G
A♭/G♯
Other Chords

X

7

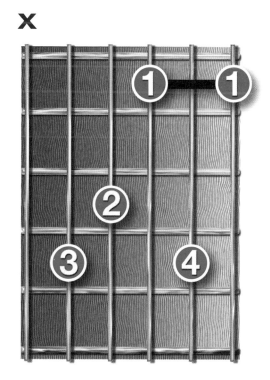

Chord Spelling

1st (G), 3rd (B), 5th (D), 9th (A)

Gm+9
Minor Add 9th

(1st position)

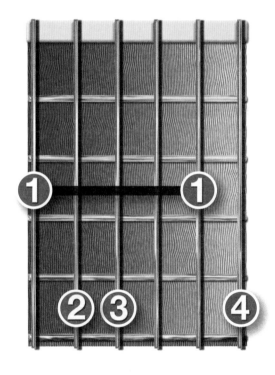

Chord Spelling

1st (G), ♭3rd (B♭), 5th (D), 9th (A)

A

B♭/A♯

B

C

C♯/D♭

D

E♭/D♯

E

F

F♯/G♭

G

A♭/G♯

Other Chords

Gm+9

Minor Add 9th

(2nd position)

X   X

7

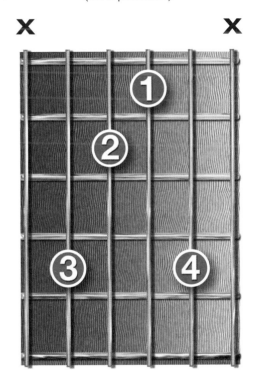

A

B♭/A♯

B

C

C♯/D♭

D

E♭/D♯

E

F

F♯/G♭

G

A♭/G♯

Other Chords

Chord Spelling

1st (G), ♭3rd (B♭), 5th (D), 9th (A)

Gm6+9

Minor 6th Add 9th

(1st position)

Chord Spelling

1st (G), ♭3rd (B♭), 5th (D), 6th (E)
9th (A)

Gm6+9

Minor 6th Add 9th

(2nd position)

A
B♭/A♯
B
C
C♯/D♭
D
E♭/D♯
E
F
F♯/G♭
G
A♭/G♯
Other Chords

X   X

8

Chord Spelling

1st (G), ♭3rd (B♭), 5th (D), 6th (E)
9th (A)

G7+9

7th Add 9th

(1st position)

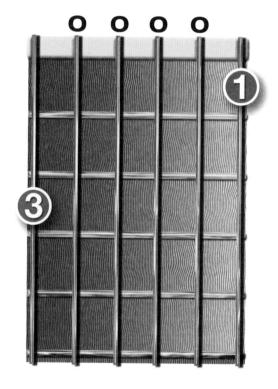

Chord Spelling

1st (G), 3rd (B), 5th (D), 7th (F#)
9th (A)

G7+9

7th Add 9th

(2nd position)

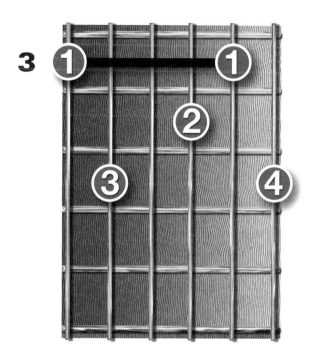

A

B♭/A♯

B

C

C♯/D♭

D

E♭/D♯

E

F

F♯/G♭

G

A♭/G♯

Other Chords

3

Chord Spelling

1st (G), 3rd (B), 5th (D), 7th (F♯)
9th (A)

G6sus4

6th Suspended 4th

(1st position)

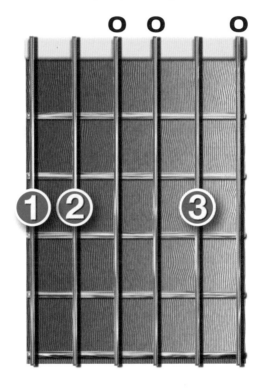

Chord Spelling

1st (G), 4th (C), 5th (D), 6th (E)

G6sus4

6th Suspended 4th

(2nd position)

Chord Spelling

1st (G), 4th (C), 5th (D), 6th (E)

A
B♭/A♯
B
C
C♯/D♭
D
E♭/D♯
E
F
F♯/G♭
G
A♭/G♯
Other Chords

A

Bb/A#

B

C

C#/Db

D

Eb/D#

E

F

F#/Gb

G

Ab/G#

Other
Chords

Gmaj7sus4

Major 7th Suspended 4th

(1st position)

Chord Spelling

1st (G), 4th (C), 5th (D), 7th (F#)

Gmaj7sus4

Major 7th Suspended 4th

(2nd position)

3

A
B♭/A♯
B
C
C♯/D♭
D
E♭/D♯
E
F
F♯/G♭
G
A♭/G♯
Other Chords

Chord Spelling

1st (G), 4th (C), 5th (D), 7th (F♯)

A

B♭/A♯

B

C

C♯/D♭

D

E♭/D♯

E

F

F♯/G♭

G

A♭/G♯

Other
Chords

Gmaj9sus4
Major 9th Suspended 4th

(1st position)

Chord Spelling

1st (G), 4th (C), 5th (D), 7th (F♯)
9th (A)

Gmaj9sus4

Major 9th Suspended 4th

(2nd position)

X

10

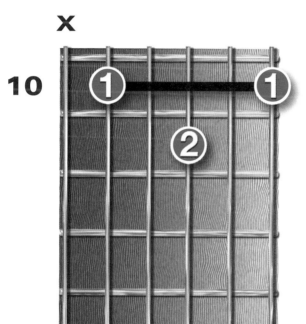

A
B♭/A#
B
C
C#/D♭
D
E♭/D#
E
F
F#/G♭
G
A♭/G#
Other Chords

Chord Spelling

1st (G), 4th (C), 5th (D), 7th (F#)
9th (A)

G9sus4

9th Suspended 4th

(1st position)

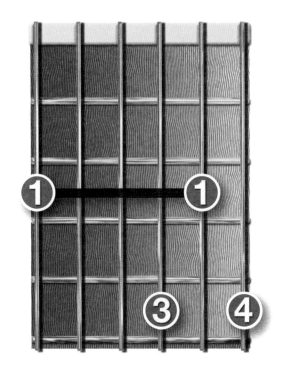

Chord Spelling

1st (G), 4th (C), 5th (D), ♭7th (F)
9th (A)

G9sus4

9th Suspended 4th

(2nd position)

A

B♭/A♯

B

C

C♯/D♭

D

E♭/D♯

E

F

F♯/G♭

G

A♭/G♯

Other Chords

X

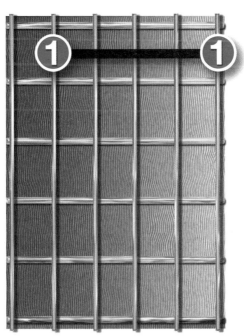

10

Chord Spelling

1st (G), 4th (C), 5th (D), ♭7th (F)
9th (A)

A♭sus2

Suspended 2nd

(1st position)

Chord Spelling

1st (A♭), 2nd (B♭), 5th (E♭)

A♭sus2

Suspended 2nd

(2nd position)

X X

6

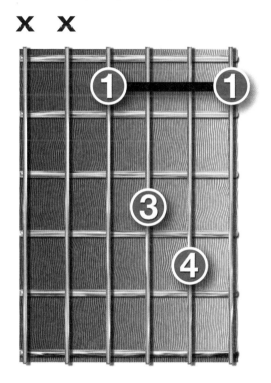

Chord Spelling

1st (A♭), 2nd (B♭), 5th (E♭)

A
B♭/A#
B
C
C#/D♭
D
E♭/D#
E
F
F#/G♭
G
A♭/G#
Other Chords

A♭maj11

Major 11th

(1st position)

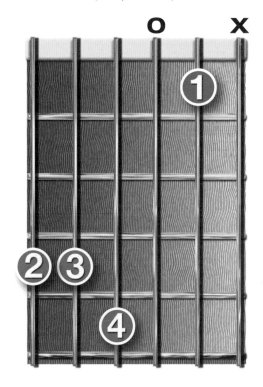

Chord Spelling

1st (A♭), 3rd (C), 5th (E♭), 7th (G),
9th (B♭), 11th (D♭)

A

B♭/A#

B

C

C#/D♭

D

E♭/D#

E

F

F#/G♭

G

A♭/G#

Other
Chords

A♭maj11

Major 11th

(2nd position)

X

8

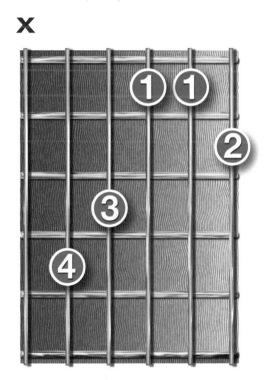

Chord Spelling

1st (A♭), 3rd (C), 5th (E♭), 7th (G),
9th (B♭), 11th (D♭)

A

B♭/A#

B

C

C#/D♭

D

E♭/D#

E

F

F#/G♭

G

A♭/G#

Other
Chords

A

B♭/A♯

B

C

C♯/D♭

D

E♭/D♯

E

F

F♯/G♭

G

A♭/G♯

Other
Chords

A♭m11
Minor 11th

(1st position)

Chord Spelling

1st (A♭), ♭3rd (C♭), 5th (E♭), ♭7th (G♭),
9th (B♭), 11th (D♭)

A♭m11

Minor 11th

(2nd position)

A

B♭/A#

B

C

C#/D♭

D

E♭/D#

E

F

F#/G♭

G

A♭/G#

Other Chords

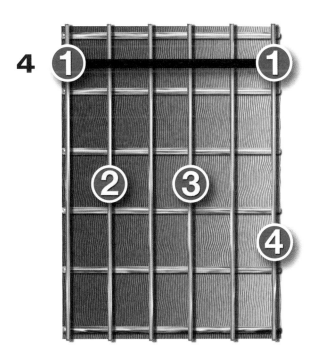

4

Chord Spelling

1st (A♭), ♭3rd (C♭), 5th (E♭), ♭7th (G♭), 9th (B♭), 11th (D♭)

A

B♭/A♯

B

C

C♯/D♭

D

E♭/D♯

E

F

F♯/G♭

G

A♭/G♯

Other Chords

A♭m maj11

Minor Major 11th

(1st position)

X

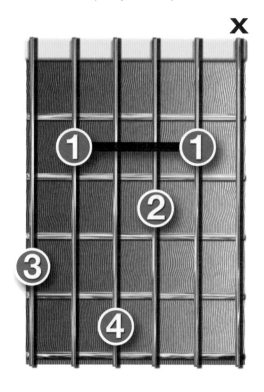

Chord Spelling

1st (A♭), ♭3rd (C♭), 5th (E♭), 7th (G)
9th (B♭), 11th (D♭)

A♭m maj11

Minor Major 11th

(2nd position)

X

9

Chord Spelling

1st (A♭), ♭3rd (C♭), 5th (E♭), 7th (G)
9th (B♭), 11th (D♭)

A

B♭/A#

B

C

C#/D♭

D

E♭/D#

E

F

F#/G♭

G

A♭/G#

Other Chords

A♭maj13
Major 13th
(1st position)

3

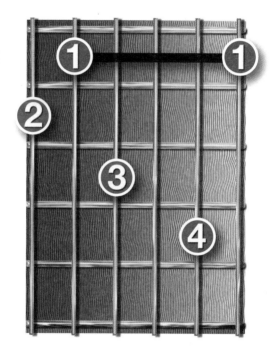

Chord Spelling

1st (A♭), 3rd (C), 5th (E♭), 7th (G)
9th (B♭), 11th (D♭), 13th (F)

A♭maj13

Major 13th

(2nd position)

X

10

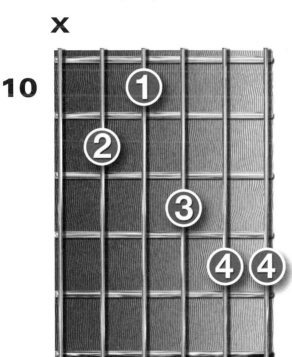

A

B♭/A♯

B

C

C♯/D♭

D

E♭/D♯

E

F

F♯/G♭

G

A♭/G♯

Other Chords

Chord Spelling

1st (A♭), 3rd (C), 5th (E♭), 7th (G)
9th (B♭), 11th (D♭), 13th (F)

A♭m13

Minor 13th

(1st position)

A

B♭/A#

B

C

C#/D♭

D

E♭/D#

E

F

F#/G♭

G

A♭/G#

Other Chords

4

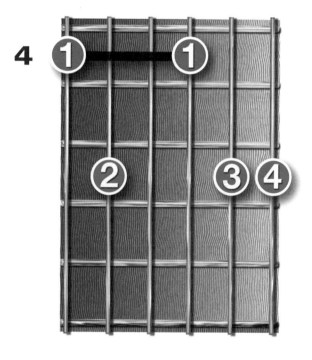

Chord Spelling

1st (A♭), ♭3rd (C♭), 5th (E♭), ♭7th (G♭)
9th (B♭), 11th (D♭), 13th (F)

A♭m13

Minor 13th

(2nd position)

X

11

A

B♭/A♯

B

C

C♯/D♭

D

E♭/D♯

E

F

F♯/G♭

G

A♭/G♯

Other Chords

Chord Spelling

1st (A♭), ♭3rd (C♭), 5th (E♭), ♭7th (G♭)
9th (B♭), 11th (D♭), 13th (F)

A

Bb/A#

B

C

C#/Db

D

Eb/D#

E

F

F#/Gb

G

Ab/G#

Other
Chords

Abm maj13
Minor Major 13th
(1st position)

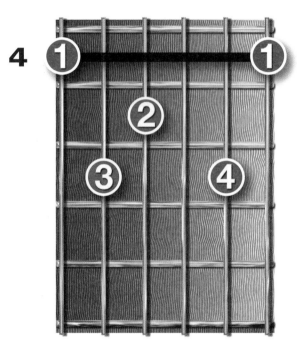

Chord Spelling
1st (Ab), b3rd (Cb), 5th (Eb), 7th (G)
9th (Bb), 11th (Db), 13th (F)

A♭m maj13

Minor Major 13th

(2nd position)

X

11

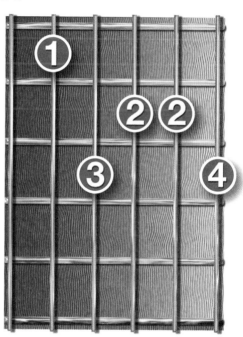

Chord Spelling

1st (A♭), ♭3rd (C♭), 5th (E♭), 7th (G)
9th (B♭), 11th (D♭), 13th (F)

A
B♭/A♯
B
C
C♯/D♭
D
E♭/D♯
E
F
F♯/G♭
G
A♭/G♯
Other Chords

A♭+9

Major Add 9th

(1st position)

Chord Spelling

1st (A♭), 3rd (C), 5th (E♭), 9th (B♭)

A

B♭/A♯

B

C

C♯/D♭

D

E♭/D♯

E

F

F♯/G♭

G

A♭/G♯

Other Chords

A♭+9

Major Add 9th

(2nd position)

X X

4

A

B♭/A♯

B

C

C♯/D♭

D

E♭/D♯

E

F

F♯/G♭

G

A♭/G♯

Other Chords

Chord Spelling

1st (A♭), 3rd (C), 5th (E♭), 9th (B♭)

A♭m + 9

Minor Add 9th

(1st position)

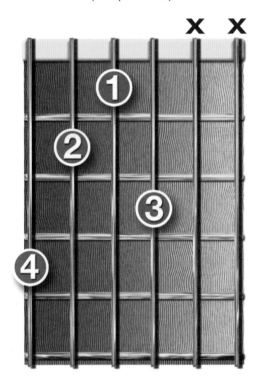

Chord Spelling

1st (A♭), ♭3rd (C♭), 5th (E♭), 9th (B♭)

A

B♭/A♯

B

C

C♯/D♭

D

E♭/D♯

E

F

F♯/G♭

G

A♭/G♯

Other
Chords

A♭m+9

Minor Add 9th

(2nd position)

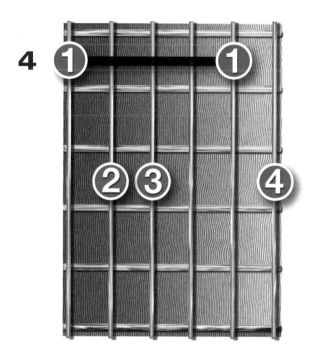

A

B♭/A♯

B

C

C♯/D♭

D

E♭/D♯

E

F

F♯/G♭

G

A♭/G♯

Other Chords

4

Chord Spelling

1st (A♭), ♭3rd (C♭), 5th (E♭), 9th (B♭)

A♭m6+9

Minor 6th Add 9th

(1st position)

X

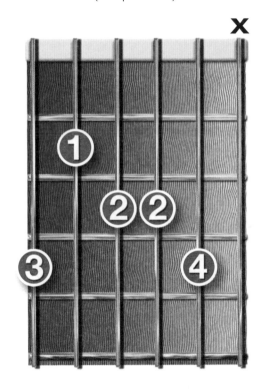

Chord Spelling

1st (A♭), ♭3rd (C♭), 5th (E♭), 6th (F)
9th (B♭)

A♭m6+9

Minor 6th Add 9th

(2nd position)

A

B♭/A#

B

C

C#/D♭

D

E♭/D#

E

F

F#/G♭

G

A♭/G#

Other Chords

X X

4

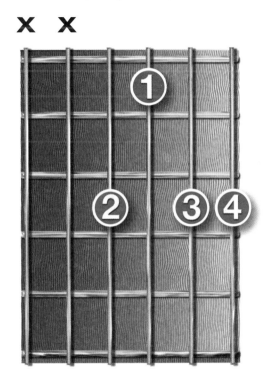

Chord Spelling

1st (A♭), ♭3rd (C♭), 5th (E♭), 6th (F)
9th (B♭)

A♭7+9

7th Add 9th

(1st position)

Chord Spelling

1st (A♭), 3rd (C), 5th (E♭), 7th (G)
9th (B♭)

A

B♭/A#

B

C

C#/D♭

D

E♭/D#

E

F

F#/G♭

G

A♭/G#

Other Chords

A♭7+9

7th Add 9th

(2nd position)

A
B♭/A#
B
C
C#/D♭
D
E♭/D#
E
F
F#/G♭
G
A♭/G#
Other Chords

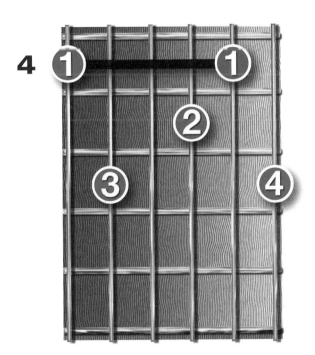

4

Chord Spelling

1st (A♭), 3rd (C), 5th (E♭), 7th (G)
9th (B♭)

A♭6sus4
6th Suspended 4th
(1st position)

Chord Spelling
1st (A♭), 4th (D♭), 5th (E♭), 6th (F)

A♭6sus4

6th Suspended 4th

(2nd position)

A

B♭/A♯

B

C

C♯/D♭

D

E♭/D♯

E

F

F♯/G♭

G

A♭/G♯

Other Chords

X   X

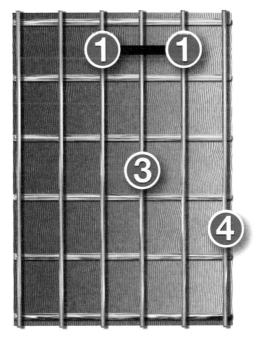

6

Chord Spelling

1st (A♭), 4th (D♭), 5th (E♭), 6th (F)

A♭maj7sus4

Major 7th Suspended 4th

(1st position)

A
B♭/A♯
B
C
C♯/D♭
D
E♭/D♯
E
F
F♯/G♭
G
A♭/G♯
Other Chords

X X X

Chord Spelling

1st (A♭), 4th (D♭), 5th (E♭), 7th (G)

A♭maj7sus4
Major 7th Suspended 4th

(2nd position)

A
B♭/A♯
B
C
C♯/D♭
D
E♭/D♯
E
F
F♯/G♭
G
A♭/G♯
Other Chords

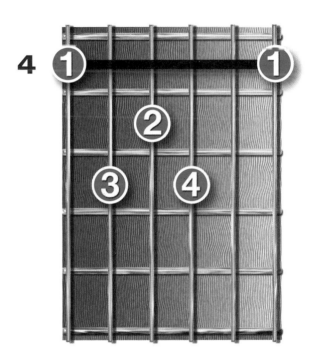

4

Chord Spelling

1st (A♭), 4th (D♭), 5th (E♭), 7th (G)

A

B♭/A#

B

C

C#/D♭

D

E♭/D#

E

F

F#/G♭

G

A♭/G#

Other Chords

A♭maj9sus4

Major 9th Suspended 4th

(1st position)

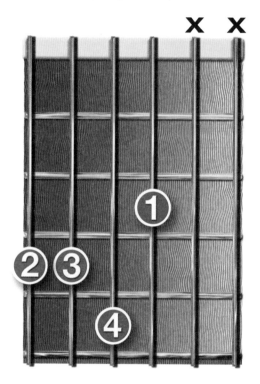

Chord Spelling

1st (A♭), 4th (D♭), 5th (E♭), 7th (G)
9th (B♭)

A♭maj9sus4
Major 9th Suspended 4th
(2nd position)

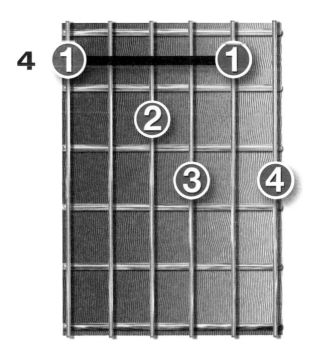

4

A

B♭/A#

B

C

C#/D♭

D

E♭/D#

E

F

F#/G♭

G

A♭/G#

Other Chords

Chord Spelling

1st (A♭), 4th (D♭), 5th (E♭), 7th (G)
9th (B♭)

A♭9sus4

9th Suspended 4th

(1st position)

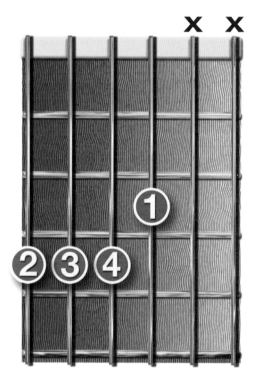

Chord Spelling

1st (A♭), 4th (D♭), 5th (E♭), ♭7th (G♭)
9th (B♭)

A

B♭/A#

B

C

C#/D♭

D

E♭/D#

E

F

F#/G♭

G

A♭/G#

Other
Chords

A♭9sus4

9th Suspended 4th

(2nd position)

A

B♭/A#

B

C

C#/D♭

D

E♭/D#

E

F

F#/G♭

G

A♭/G#

Other Chords

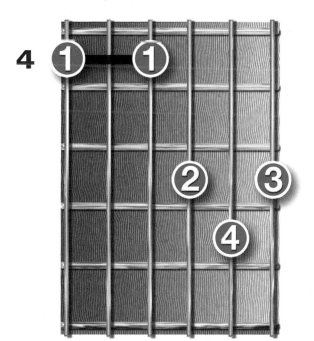

4

Chord Spelling

1st (A♭), 4th (D♭), 5th (E♭), ♭7th (G♭)
9th (B♭)

A

B♭/A♯

B

C

C♯/D♭

D

E♭/D♯

E

F

F♯/G♭

G

A♭/G♯

Other Chords

Am maj7
Minor Major 7th
(1st position)

Chord Spelling
1st (A), ♭3rd (C), 5th (E), 7th (G♯)

Am maj9
Minor Major 9th
(1st position)

Chord Spelling
1st (A), ♭3rd (C), 5th (E), 7th (G♯), 9th (B)

Amaj7+5
Augmented Major 7th
(1st position)

Chord Spelling
1st (A), 3rd (C♯), ♯5th (F), 7th (G♯)

A+7
Augmented 7th
(1st position)

Chord Spelling
1st (A), 3rd (C♯), ♯5th (F), ♭7th (G)

B♭m maj7
Minor Major 7th
(1st position)

Chord Spelling
1st (B♭), ♭3rd (D♭), 5th (F), 7th (A)

B♭m maj9
Minor Major 9th
(1st position)

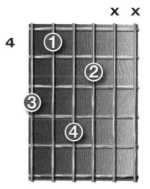

Chord Spelling
1st (B♭), ♭3rd (D♭), 5th (F), 7th (A), 9th (C)

B♭maj7+5
Augmented Major 7th
(1st position)

Chord Spelling
1st (B♭), 3rd (D), #5th (F#), 7th (A)

B♭+7
Augmented 7th
(1st position)

Chord Spelling
1st (B♭), 3rd (D), #5th (F#), ♭7th (G#)

A
B♭/A#
B
C
C#/D♭
D
E♭/D#
E
F
F#/G♭
G
A♭/G#
Other Chords

A
Bb/A#
B
C
C#/Db
D
Eb/D#
E
F
F#/Gb
G
Ab/G#
Other
Chords

Bm maj7
Minor Major 7th
(1st position)

Chord Spelling
1st (B), ♭3rd (D), 5th (F#), 7th (A#)

Bm maj9
Minor Major 9th
(1st position)

Chord Spelling
1st (B), ♭3rd (D), 5th (F#), 7th (A#), 9th (C#)

Bmaj7+5
Augmented Major 7th
(1st position)

Chord Spelling
1st (B), 3rd (D#), #5th (G), 7th (A#)

B+7
Augmented 7th
(1st position)

Chord Spelling
1st (B), 3rd (D#), #5th (G), ♭7th (A)

Cm maj7
Minor Major 7th
(1st position)

Chord Spelling
1st (C), ♭3rd (E♭), 5th (G), 7th (B)

Cm maj9
Minor Major 9th
(1st position)

Chord Spelling
1st (C), ♭3rd (E♭), 5th (G), 7th (B), 9th (D)

Cmaj7+5
Augmented Major 7th
(1st position)

Chord Spelling
1st (C), 3rd (E), ♯5th (G♯), 7th (B)

C+7
Augmented 7th
(1st position)

Chord Spelling
1st (C), 3rd (E), ♯5th (G♯), ♭7th (B♭)

A
B♭/A♯
B
C
C♯/D♭
D
E♭/D♯
E
F
F♯/G♭
G
A♭/G♯
Other Chords

C#m maj7
Minor Major 7th
(1st position)

Chord Spelling
1st (C#), b3rd (E), 5th (G#), 7th (B#)

C#m maj9
Minor Major 9th
(1st position)

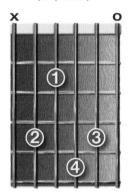

Chord Spelling
1st (C#), b3rd (E), 5th (G#), 7th (B#), 9th (D#)

C#maj7+5
Augmented Major 7th
(1st position)

Chord Spelling
1st (C#), 3rd (E#), #5th (A), 7th (B#)

C#+7
Augmented 7th
(1st position)

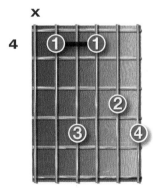

Chord Spelling
1st (C#), 3rd (E#), #5th (A), b7th (B)

Dm maj7
Minor Major 7th
(1st position)

Chord Spelling
1st (D), ♭3rd (F), 5th (A), 7th (C♯)

Dm maj9
Minor Major 9th
(1st position)

Chord Spelling
1st (D), ♭3rd (F), 5th (A), 7th (C♯), 9th (E)

Dmaj7+5
Augmented Major 7th
(1st position)

Chord Spelling
1st (D), 3rd (F♯), ♯5th (A♯), 7th (C♯)

D+7
Augmented 7th
(1st position)

Chord Spelling
1st (xD), 3rd (F♯), ♯5th (A♯), ♭7th (C)

A
B♭/A♯
B
C
C♯/D♭
D
E♭/D♯
E
F
F♯/G♭
G
A♭/G♯
Other Chords

E♭m maj7
Minor Major 7th
(1st position)

Chord Spelling
1st (E♭), ♭3rd (G♭), 5th (B♭), 7th (D)

E♭m maj9
Minor Major 9th
(1st position)

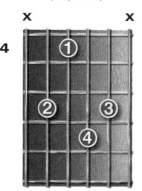

Chord Spelling
1st (E♭), ♭3rd (G♭), 5th (B♭), 7th (D), 9th (F)

E♭maj7+5
Augmented Major 7th
(1st position)

Chord Spelling
1st (E♭), 3rd (G), ♯5th (B), 7th (D)

E♭+7
Augmented 7th
(1st position)

Chord Spelling
1st (E♭), 3rd (G), ♯5th (B), ♭7th (D♭)

A
B♭/A♯
B
C
C♯/D♭
D
E♭/D♯
E
F
F♯/G♭
G
A♭/G♯
Other Chords

Em maj7
Minor Major 7th
(1st position)

Chord Spelling
1st (E), ♭3rd (G), 5th (B), 7th (D♯)

Em maj9
Minor Major 9th
(1st position)

Chord Spelling
1st (E), ♭3rd (G), 5th (B), 7th (D♯), 9th (F♯)

Emaj7+5
Augmented Major 7th
(1st position)

Chord Spelling
1st (E), 3rd (G♯), ♯5th (B♯), 7th (D♯)

E+7
Augmented 7th
(1st position)

Chord Spelling
1st (E), 3rd (G♯), ♯5th (B♯), ♭7th (D)

A
B♭/A♯
B
C
C♯/D♭
D
E♭/D♯
E
F
F♯/G♭
G
A♭/G♯
Other Chords

A

B♭/A#

B

C

C#/D♭

D

E♭/D#

E

F

F#/G♭

G

A♭/G#

Other Chords

Fm maj7
Minor Major 7th
(1st position)

Chord Spelling
1st (F), ♭3rd (A♭), 5th (C), 7th (E)

Fm maj9
Minor Major 9th
(1st position)

Chord Spelling
1st (F), ♭3rd (A♭), 5th (C), 7th (E), 9th (G)

Fmaj7+5
Augmented Major 7th
(1st position)

Chord Spelling
1st (F), 3rd (A), #5th (C#), 7th (E)

F+7
Augmented 7th
(1st position)

Chord Spelling
1st (F), 3rd (A), #5th (C#), ♭7th (D#)

F#m maj7
Minor Major 7th
(1st position)

Chord Spelling
1st (F#), b3rd (A), 5th (C#), 7th (E#)

F#m maj9
Minor Major 9th
(1st position)

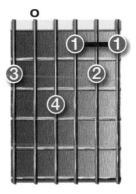

Chord Spelling
1st (F#), b3rd (A), 5th (C#), 7th (E#), 9th (G#)

F#maj7+5
Augmented Major 7th
(1st position)

Chord Spelling
1st (F#), 3rd (A#), #5th (D), 7th (E#)

F#+7
Augmented 7th
(1st position)

Chord Spelling
1st (F#), 3rd (A#), #5th (D), b7th (E)

A
Bb/A#
B
C
C#/Db
D
Eb/D#
E
F
F#/Gb
G
Ab/G#
Other Chords

Gm maj7
Minor Major 7th
(1st position)

Chord Spelling
1st (G), ♭3rd (B♭), 5th (D), 7th (F♯)

Gm maj9
Minor Major 9th
(1st position)

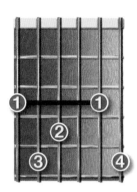

Chord Spelling
1st (G), ♭3rd (B♭), 5th (D), 7th (F♯), 9th (A)

Gmaj7+5
Augmented Major 7th
(1st position)

Chord Spelling
1st (G), 3rd (B), ♯5th (D♯), 7th (F♯)

G+7
Augmented 7th
(1st position)

Chord Spelling
1st (G), 3rd (B), ♯5th (D♯), ♭7th (F)

A
B♭/A♯
B
C
C♯/D♭
D
E♭/D♯
E
F
F♯/G♭
G
A♭/G♯
Other Chords

A♭m maj7
Minor Major 7th
(1st position)

Chord Spelling
1st (A♭), ♭3rd (B), 5th (E♭), 7th (G)

A♭m maj9
Minor Major 9th
(1st position)

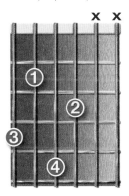

Chord Spelling
1st (A♭), ♭3rd (B), 5th (E♭), 7th (G), 9th (B♭)

A♭maj7+5
Augmented Major 7th
(1st position)

Chord Spelling
1st (A♭), 3rd (C), ♯5th (E), 7th (G)

A♭+7
Augmented 7th
(1st position)

Chord Spelling
1st (A♭), 3rd (C), ♯5th (E), ♭7th (G♭)

A
B♭/A♯
B
C
C♯/D♭
D
E♭/D♯
E
F
F♯/G♭
G
A♭/G♯
Other Chords

Chord Spelling Reference

Scale of A Major

A	B	C#	D	E	F#	G#
1st	2nd	3rd	4th	5th	6th	7th
	9th		11th		13th	

Scale of B♭/A# Major

B♭	C	D	E♭	F	G	A
1st	2nd	3rd	4th	5th	6th	7th
	9th		11th		13th	

Scale of B Major

B	C#	D#	E	F#	G#	A#
1st	2nd	3rd	4th	5th	6th	7th
	9th		11th		13th	

A

B♭/A#

B

C

C#/D♭

D

E♭/D#

E

F

F#/G♭

G

A♭/G#

Other
Chords

Scale of C Major

C	D	E	F	G	A	B
1st	2nd	3rd	4th	5th	6th	7th
	9th		11th		13th	

Scale of C#/D♭ Major

C#	D#	E#	F#	G#	A#	B#
1st	2nd	3rd	4th	5th	6th	7th
	9th		11th		13th	

Scale of D Major

D	E	F#	G	A	B	C#
1st	2nd	3rd	4th	5th	6th	7th
	9th		11th		13th	

Scale of E♭/D♯ Major

E♭	F	G	A♭	B♭	C	D
1st	2nd	3rd	4th	5th	6th	7th
	9th		11th		13th	

Scale of E Major

E	F♯	G♯	A	B	C♯	D♯
1st	2nd	3rd	4th	5th	6th	7th
	9th		11th		13th	

Scale of F Major

F	G	A	B♭	C	D	E
1st	2nd	3rd	4th	5th	6th	7th
	9th		11th		13th	

A
B♭/A♯
B
C
C♯/D♭
D
E♭/D♯
E
F
F♯/G♭
G
A♭/G♯
Other Chords

Scale of F#/G♭ Major

F#	G#	A#	B	C#	D#	E#
1st	2nd	3rd	4th	5th	6th	7th
	9th		11th		13th	

Scale of G Major

G	A	B	C#	D	E	F#
1st	2nd	3rd	4th	5th	6th	7th
	9th		11th		13th	

Scale of A♭/G# Major

A♭	B♭	C	D♭	E♭	F	G
1st	2nd	3rd	4th	5th	6th	7th
	9th		11th		13th	

A

B♭/A#

B

C

C#/D♭

D

E♭/D#

E

F

F#/G♭

G

A♭/G#

Other
Chords

FLAME TREE | PUBLISHING
MUSIC PORTAL

Hear Chords and Scales
FLAMETREEMUSIC.COM

Expert Music Information
FLAMETREEPRO.COM

Sheet Music Playlists
FLAMETREEPIANO.COM

The **FLAME TREE MUSIC PORTAL** brings **chords** and **scales** you can see *and* hear, an **Expert Music search engine** on a wide range of genres, styles, artists and instruments, and free access to **playlists** for our sheet music series.

Other FLAME TREE music books include:

Guitar Chords by Jake Jackson
Piano & Keyboard Chords by Jake Jackson
Beginners Guide to Reading Music by Jake Jackson
The Jazz and Blues Encyclopedia (Editor: Howard Mandel)
Definitive Opera Encyclopedia (Founding Editor: Stanley Sadie)
Sheet Music for Piano: Scott Joplin by Alan Brown

See our full range of books at **flametreepublishing.com**